TEA AND ME

A Memoir of Planting Life

E S J DAVIDAR

EastWest Books (Madras) Pvt Ltd

● Chennai ● Mumbai ● Bangalore ● Hyderabad ● New Delhi

EastWest Books (Madras) Pvt Ltd
571, Poonamallee High Road, Kamaraj Bhavan, Aminjikarai, Chennai - 600 029.
I Floor, Praja Bhavan, 53/2 Bull Temple Road, Basavangudi, Bangalore - 560 019.
I Floor, 3-5-1108 Maruthi Complex, Narayanaguda, Hyderabad - 500 029.
Plot No.102, Marol Coop Ind Estate, Marol, Andheri East, Mumbai - 400 059.
F-5 Okhla Industrial Area, Phase-1, Mezzanine Floor, New Delhi - 110 020.

Copyright © 2008 E S J Davidar

ISBN 13: 978-81-88661-71-8

Cover design
J Menon, www.cantocorp.com/design

Typeset in Palatino Linotype

Printed at
Saibonds Print Systems Pvt Ltd, Chennai - 600 094
E-mail: saiprints@saimail.com

Published by
EastWest Books (Madras) Pvt Ltd
571, Poonamallee High Road, Kamaraj Bhavan,
Aminjikarai, Chennai - 600 029
E-mail: ewb@ewbpl.com

In loving memory of my wife
Susie
who had immense faith in me
and for

Lt Col JRP Williams, MBE

a true officer and gentleman

There is one thing that is stronger than all the armies of the world and that is an idea whose time has come

Victor Hugo

There is a time for everything

Ecclesiastes 3:1

Contents

Preface vii

Introduction xi

PART ONE

The Romance of Tea 3

Early Days 18

Of Geese and General Managers 26

Ghosts, Snakes and Labour Trouble 32

Birds in Trees and Fireflies at Night 49

Malabar Police and Spies 54

Passage to London 67

Death on the Estate 81

The Burning Bungalow 89

Tackling the Unions 93

Ascending the Gaddi 110

Impending Change 117

The Old Order Changeth 129

Finis 132

PART TWO

Adventures in Shikar 145

Directors' Foibles 161

On Two Wheels and Four 172

Days and Nights at the Club 182

Gentlemen's Gentlemen 190

A Question of Colour 198

Epilogue 203

Appendix 206

Acknowledgements 212

Select Bibliography 215

Preface

When I first attempted to write my memoirs in 1985, I opened with the sentence that planters and their wives who had lived in plantation districts like Peermade, while leading lives of quiet desperation, have been heard to say that at the end of it all they could probably write a book about their varied experiences. I was very pleased to have coined the phrase 'leading lives of quiet desperation' but I soon abandoned that first effort when a publisher I showed some pages to suggested I turn the book into a work of fiction. You can either write a novel or you can't, and I belong in the latter category.

Exactly twenty years later, when I made the next attempt, I happened to read *Walden*, the classic written by the American essayist David Henry Thoreau a century and a half ago. Midway through the book, I was startled to see that Thoreau had written that 'most men lead lives of quiet desperation'. I felt gratified that I could produce a sentence like the great Thoreau, but was even more struck by the fact that 'leading lives of desperation' existed down the ages, not just among the planters in Peermade.

Mine is not the first contemporary account of tea planting life in South India; that distinction must go to Heather Lovatt, an Englishwoman, whose husband, John, was a planter in the same area that I worked in. When the idea of a book first occurred to me, I wrote about my plans to Heather, who with her husband had long retired to the United Kingdom. Heather wrote back to say that she had a good laugh but thought at the same time that it could be interesting to see planting life through my eyes.

Before they left the district for good, Heather told me in the Club one evening that at various times, she had entertained the thought of writing a book on planting life but had never got around to doing so. However, she wrote a treatise entitled, *Peermade – Vandiperiyar, A Short History,* while they were still in India, and it was eventually published as a book called, *Above The Heron's Pool*, which was edited by a her friend Peter de Jong who was once the Chief Scientific Officer of The United Planters' Association of Southern India (UPASI) in The Nilgiris.

My son, David (aka Jai), became a publisher with Penguin Books in 1985. On his visits to England, he met or chatted on the telephone with Heather or members of her family. After one such conversation, Heather wrote to me and said that it was a great idea that I should write a book about my time in planting. She went on to say that she had suggested to my son on the telephone that she and I could collaborate on a book. Nothing came of the idea because soon after writing that letter (in September 1989), Heather, sadly, developed cancer of the pancreas and passed away within a year.

However, I didn't give up hope, not yet. On the premise that I might eventually write a book about my life in tea, I kept notes of various incidents that I felt might make interesting reading. But I would never have imagined that I would only get around to writing this book when I turned 80. The credit should go entirely to Usha Joseph. I have known Usha and her husband George (who was a planter in my district with Travancore Tea Estates Company – TTE) for many years. Although based in Bangalore, some years ago they bought themselves a nice house in Coonoor – a few miles from Wellington where I live – to get away to the hills every now and then. From the time that I started seeing them in Coonoor, Usha suggested that I should write a book about my planting life. She became more and more insistent with each succeeding visit and I finally decided to give in. My daughter, Ruth (aka Lulu), also felt that some of the stories that I told her about my life in Peermade were worth recording for posterity, and urged me to start writing. When my son, David (who is himself an author), heard about my intentions and saw a bit of sample writing, he said I should go ahead and offered to edit the book when it was finished.

At about this time I was reminded of an article entitled, *The View from 80* by Malcolm Cowley, that distinguished man of letters, which I had read many years previously in *Life* magazine. I was so struck by Cowley's trenchant observations that I wrote down the entire article without having the faintest idea at the time that I would live to see 80. Anyway, one of the insights Cowley proffered in his article was that every old person needs a work project to keep more alive. He went on to say that rereading old letters and fitting together memories could lead to writing a book of memoirs.

My first Chairman, Col JRP Williams, kept up his personal correspondence with my wife, Susie, and myself until practically the end of his life, despite the massive stroke which left his right side paralysed. He taught himself to write again, even if it was only a scrawl. He wrote and told us when he was in his seventies that he was writing his life story which was not for publication. He was a methodical man, and he said in his letter that the pocket diaries which he had kept for over thirty years had helped him to recollect people, places and events. So, it is not entirely strange that people should want to write about their lives, especially in their old age.

In this account of life in a tea district, I hope readers will get a glimpse of the transition that followed India's Independence when a sterling Company which employed only men from the United Kingdom came to be wholly managed by an Indian.

∽

Introduction

Tea has had a long and storied history. It was discovered in China centuries ago. Battles have been fought over it; all sorts of qualities attributed to it; and for hundreds of years, it was the world's most popular beverage. In India, Robert Bruce, a Scotsman (most of the early planters were Scots), is credited with the discovery of tea plants in the jungles of Upper Assam in 1823.

Robert (later to become a Major in the Bengal Artillery) was a trader who had set up business in Assam. His younger brother, Charles, was in command of a division of British Gunboats in Upper Assam when the Burmese War broke out in May 1824. The Bruce brothers married local women, and had settled down in Assam when Robert chanced upon the tea plants.

Robert Bruce was an adventurer and a true mercenary. He'd first fight on one side, and when it suited him, he would switch over to the side of the erstwhile enemy, all for his own benefit. Unfortunately, we don't know when he died, but before he passed on, he had told Charles about the tea plants.

In 1828, Charles Bruce sent a bouquet of tea to the Governor-General's Agent, and wrote a letter to the Agent in 1836 saying that his late brother, Robert Bruce, who was in Assam before the start of the Burmese War, had informed him of the existence of tea plants. His claim to have discovered the indigenous tea plants led to the establishment of the Assam Company in 1839. Charles Bruce was appointed the first Superintendent of the tea estates of the Company.

Lieutenant Andrew Charlton of the Assam Light Infantry fiercely disputed Charles Bruce's claim that he was the first to discover the tea plant in Assam. Charlton claimed in his letter to the Governor-General's Agent that he was the first to find tea plants in Assam as far back as in 1831, when he had sent them to the Agri-Horticultural Society of Calcutta. Both Charles Bruce and Andrew Charlton received awards for 'discovering' tea plants growing wild in Assam, but from different organizations. The Royal Society of Arts in London honoured Charles Bruce with a medal in 1840, while Andrew Charlton was awarded a medal by the Agri-Horticultural Society in Calcutta in support of his claim to be the discoverer of tea plants in Assam. One of the ironies of the tea business in India is that the real discoverer of the plant, Robert Bruce, died without any honour being conferred on him, while others received recognition.

With the discovery of tea in Assam, several tea estates came into being, slowly at first and too rapidly for comfort later. Dishonest practices crept in, and estates, some of which were estates only in name, were sold at many times their real worth. The men who were recruited to run the estates were a motley crowd. There were ordinary seamen, retired or cashiered Army and Navy officers, shopkeepers of all kinds, stable keepers, and disreputable men who hadn't made good in other jobs. They were nearly all totally ignorant of tea planting, and the end was inevitable. Only the estates that were properly established and carefully managed survived.

Even the Assam Company, which was formed in 1839 and led the revolution in growing tea on a commercial scale, was no exception to bad management. Money was spent recklessly with the imminent prospect of making huge fortunes, but no worthwhile progress was made. Weeds proliferated to such an extent that the tea plants could hardly be seen. A scapegoat had to be found, and Charles Bruce was sacked in 1846. Quite fortuitously, conditions started to improve the very next year, and the first genuine dividend was announced by the Company in 1852.

While the planting of tea became the rage in Assam, it did not evoke much interest in the south of the country. Coffee continued to be the favoured crop, as it brought in large sums of money and helped the owners of the coffee estates to become very rich. Where was the need then to switch to tea? In fact, the Tea Committee in Calcutta had sent tea seeds and plants to the South, but nobody took any serious interest in growing the plant on a plantation scale.

According to one version, Dr Christie, a Company Surgeon, evinced an interest in tea as it looked like the *Camellia* plant which grew well in The Nilgiris. He was the first to experiment with growing tea in the South as early as in 1832. But his death put an end to the venture. Another report has it that before the tea seeds that he had ordered could arrive, Dr Christie died. Nothing of great relevance happened for a long time afterwards, although some tea was grown in the Agricultural Farm in Ketti in The Nilgiris in 1835. Commercial planting of tea started again in The Nilgiris on the Thiashola and Dunsandle Estates around 1859, and in Kotagiri in 1863.

Tea was first introduced in Travancore in 1864, when it was planted experimentally in the Government Gardens in the hilly district of Peermade, situated at an elevation of just under four thousand feet above sea level. The tea plants flourished. But with coffee doing so well, nobody in the South was seriously interested in exploiting tea commercially.

And then, disaster struck. Coffee was the predominant plantation crop in Ceylon (as Sri Lanka was then called). The coffee leaf disease, *Hemileia vastatrix,* appeared in Ceylon in 1869. The affected leaves fell off, and new ones did not grow in their place. The yield of coffee beans also dropped dramatically. Chemical control of pests and blights was practically unknown in those days. The coffee planters tried to overcome the problem with better methods of cultivation, but the industry was doomed to failure. Many planters in Ceylon were ruined and left the island. A year or so later, the disease spread to the coffee plantations in the south of India. With coffee as a plantation crop destroyed, thoughts naturally turned to tea.

The commercial cultivation of tea first began in Travancore in the Kanan Devan Hills in 1878. It was grown on a small scale in Peermade district around 1895. A Company named Southern India Tea Estates Company Limited (SITE) was incorporated in 1897, and was one among the early tea companies that were established in Peermade and the adjoining Vandiperiyar district. The rest of this story revolves around SITE which the author joined in 1953 as an Assistant Superintendent, the first Indian Executive to be employed in that British (sterling) Company.

〜

PART ONE

The Romance of Tea

M y father, Ambrose Davidar, was the Judge in Ooty in The Nilgiris in the 1940s before India became independent. As luck would have it, a paternal uncle, Pandiaraj Davidar (who was chiefly responsible for my becoming a tea planter) was posted as the Manager of Warwick Estate in Kotagiri (also in The Nilgiris, twenty miles from Ooty) at about the same time. Warwick Estate was once owned by an English proprietary planter who sold out to the Indian plantations Company for which my uncle worked.

The law courts in India closed for two months each year in the summer. My father had a car – owning one was quite unusual in those days – a sturdy Morris-12. For a couple of years each summer, we would drive across to Kotagiri as a family to spend a week in my uncle's spacious bungalow on Warwick Estate. The bungalow had a rolling lawn and a duck pond. There was a jungle just behind the bungalow where jungle fowl called every morning. Wild guava (*Rhodomyrtus tomentosa*) grew in abundance there, and we ate the luscious fruit of the shrub until sated. I even shot a sambar in the jungle once.

I was enchanted by the bungalow with its lawn, the jungle behind it, and the wild guava fruit. But, what really captivated me was the enticing aroma of tea wafting from the rolling room of the tea factory. I decided then that I would like nothing better than to become a tea planter.

I was at university then, and when I graduated a couple of years later, my father, who was still the Judge in Ooty, helped me to apply for the job of Assistant Manager in a tea plantations Company in the Anamallais. The Company which had its Head Office in Bombay was run by European planters, and I was told that they had a young Indian Assistant on their Executive Staff.

In due course, I was called for an interview. They were not going to leave anything to chance and I was asked to stay with the General Manager of the Company for three nights. On the two days following my arrival, I was taken around their estates, on foot, by two senior Managers who were to assess my suitability or otherwise to become a fledgling planter in their Company. They were kind men, and as we walked around the estates they explained what tea planting was all about. I had lunch and tea with them, and in the evening they brought me back to the General Manager's bungalow. All three men happened to be grass widowers at the time, and it was my first experience of being the guest of Englishmen. While I wasn't exactly awed by the experience, I wasn't too sure that I was yet ready to live and work with British planters. When I received a letter from the Company's General Manager a few days after I returned home saying that Assistant Managers' jobs in their Company were rather large charges and they didn't think I was quite ready yet to join them as one, I was actually quite relieved.

After my failure to get a job as a tea planter, I stayed at home and applied for all kinds of jobs, like most other un-employed graduates did. In the days before India attained Independence, job vacancies for Executives were few. The saying was, 'Apply, apply, no reply'. It was true. There was no reply to any of the numerous applications that I sent.

And then, I joined the Indian Army in 1948. It was the only other career that appealed to me. I loved the military uniform. The first two years of my Army service were wonderful years. I served in a Sikh artillery regiment and they accepted me even though I was a Tamil and didn't know one word of Hindustani. I was affectionately known as *kaala saab* (black officer) by the *jawans*.

Most Sikh soldiers are of rural stock and their loyalty is intense. When I was going to leave, my orderly of about three years, Jothi Singh, wanted to quit the Army and come away with me to serve me permanently. It took all my powers of persuasion to dissuade him.

My regiment was posted to a small station in Bihar called Ramgarh where I was for a year. The Officers' Club was just across the road from our bachelors' quarters. Every Saturday night, all the officers and the families of the married ones met at the Club, and there was much singing and dancing. We went out on shikar every now and then. We had gone one day for a lake shoot. We were about six officers, all subalterns. Except for one shotgun (which was used mainly to shoot mongrels which strayed into the regimental area), everybody was armed with a Service rifle. With which to shoot ducks! We hadn't bagged anything and after a while we decided to get back to the Mess. All the other chaps, incidentally, were new to the game, and none of them had handled a firearm before they had joined the Army. I was, naturally then, the officer in charge of shikar.

We usually removed the tarpaulin from the back of the truck (leaving the iron superstructure bare) so that we could all stand and look for game as we passed. There was one particular occasion when I was the last but one to get in. As the last chap was about to mount, we heard a loud report. At the same time, I felt the sensation of a dozen or so pinpricks on my butt. I automatically put my hand on my backside, and felt something warm. My hand was covered in blood. The last chap getting in had accidentally pressed the trigger. The idiot hadn't unloaded his weapon on reaching the truck, a cardinal rule. Fortunately for me, the bullet from the Service rifle, on hitting the iron superstructure, ricocheted outwards and only some splinters were deflected inwards which caught me in the seat of my pants. The chaps became very concerned, and the senior subaltern present told the driver of the truck to step on it and get to the Mess as quickly as possible. When we reached the Mess, they carried me to my room and laid me on my bed. For some reason, they decided not to tell anybody, not even the Adjutant who had sanctioned the truck for us to use. Neither was I taken to the Military Hospital in the station to avoid being asked awkward questions. I think they put out the story that I was not well and was confined to bed. You never saw a more solicitous band of fellow officers. They took turns bringing me food and there was somebody standing guard much of the time. Although the Adjutant and my Battery Commander were also with us in the bachelors' quarters, neither of them came to see me. I think everybody came to know what had actually happened and had decided to keep up the joke that I was ill. I was young and with the blood running hot, I healed remarkably quickly. But for years afterwards, whenever I scratched my bottom I'd come up with a lead splinter.

My regiment was then transferred to Jhansi which was a much larger station. The Officers' Club was some distance away, but we had a squash court on our Mess grounds and I played the game nearly every evening. The shikar was excellent. A wizened little man would sit on the verandah outside my room most Saturdays when I came to my room after lunch. Every time he saw me, he said the same thing, *"Panther hai, Saab."* Not infrequently, some officers and I took a truck – it was sanctioned for reconnaissance purposes, a legitimate reason for gunners to take out a truck – and went where the little man led us. We never saw a panther though, but we shot other game. The man also took us to a huge lake, and we traversed over rough terrain for many miles. There were all kinds of waterbirds in their hundreds, including wild geese in season. We usually got to the lake by nightfall, had our packed supper and tried to sleep on the shore of the lake to the accompaniment of bird sounds, a veritable cacophony.

The Commanding Officer (CO) of the regiment, a new man, called an informal meeting of all the officers in the Mess one evening to discuss the menu for the forthcoming Artillery Day dinner, to which officers from other units in the station were to be invited and the chief guest was to be the Brigade Commander. The wild geese were still around. When he asked for everybody's views, one senior captain said we could start with 'horse devour us' (sic) and the CO said, with a straight face, "Ordevr, yes." Before anybody else could come up with other brilliant ideas, the CO, who obviously knew what he wanted, said, "Gentlemen, I would like to suggest that we have roast wild geese for the main dish." There was no dissent, naturally, and it was agreed that a day before Artillery Day a wild goose shoot would take place. The CO turned to me and said, "Davy, (by which name I was known to the officers in the regiment) will you organize the shoot?" And the meeting was adjourned.

When the time came, we set out in two trucks with a skeleton Mess staff to prepare our meals on the lake shore. We spent the night as usual beside the lake, and early the next morning, as the geese flew into the fields adjoining the lake to feed, a general fusillade rang out. Not one bird fell. By the time we gathered for breakfast – the wives of some of the officers were present as well – we were a pretty despondent lot. The CO, not much of a *shikari* himself, took the shotgun and went for a walk while we were having breakfast. We saw him disappearing round a bend in the lake and within a few minutes we heard a shot. What should we see presently but the CO dragging three fat geese behind him. He said quite simply that as he rounded the bend, he saw three geese sitting together at fairly close range, and all three fell to one shot from his gun. We had our roast geese after all for the Artillery Day dinner.

My regiment was transferred to the wheat fields of Punjab the next year. In those early days after Partition when relations between India and Pakistan were at a low ebb, we were threatened with invasion each year and it was known as 'sabre-rattling'. We lived in tents in the fields, and life as I knew it in the previous two years came to an end. We couldn't take our artillery guns out on exercise, as we used to do before, for reasons of security. All we had to do was to keep ourselves physically fit. There was no social life and no visits to other military units which were not close to us anyhow. And, there was no invasion to resist to give us some real action either. It would be difficult to describe how incredibly boring life could be with nothing worthwhile to do. Thus passed one year.

The next year, my battery was detached from the regiment and sent to Jammu to relieve another battery from another regiment on a similar mission. In the early days of Independence, there were only two medium regiments of artillery, and they were the biggest guns the Indian Army had. Almost twenty years later, when I was still with my plantations Company in Peermade, I met a dear friend, a brother officer from my old regiment, quite by accident, when he was touring by car with his family in my district. He was a Sikh, and he and his wife and children spent a night with me and my wife on the estate. I casually asked him how many medium artillery regiments were there in the Army then. He said there were so many you couldn't count them.

For the second year running, there was only idleness. And boredom. We sat around all day, and swilled whisky and played bridge at night. I was not surprised, therefore, that the old yearning to be a tea planter returned. I decided to leave the Army. That year, 1952, when I came on leave to Madras, I travelled to The Nilgiris where my uncle, Pandiaraj Davidar, was now the Manager of Sutton Estate, a beautiful property. Sutton was very close to Coonoor which was also where the office of UPASI was situated. I stayed as my uncle's guest, and he took me around in his car to meet various European planters in The Nilgiris to find out if there was any suitable billet going vacant. There was none.

Col GAR Spain, a retired British Army officer and a proprietary planter in Kotagiri, was one of the men we met. Col Spain led me into his study and proceeded to be blunt. He said there was no longer any glamour in planting and I would be well advised to stay on in the Army. I told him that it was possible only for the foreseeable future. He tut-tutted and said okay, in that case he'd do what he could to help. He sat at his typewriter and tapped out a very nice letter to an English planter friend of his asking him if he could help. He couldn't. I was sorry that I never met Col Spain again.

Some months later, though, I received a letter from my uncle Pandiaraj. Enclosed was a telegram he had received from one CJ Madden asking me to meet him for an interview at the Malabar Hotel in Cochin. What had happened was that my uncle had learnt that there was a vacancy for an Assistant Manager in a Company called Tea Estates (India) Limited, a Brooke Bond Company. He had applied on my behalf. This Company had started recruiting Indian Executives before any other English-dominated Company had decided to do so, and my uncle thought I stood a chance. Although there wasn't a job there, this initiative piqued the interest of Madden who was then the General Manager in India of SITE. Madden was looking to recruit an Indian Assistant Superintendent for his Company. He had met JLH Williams, the No.1 of Tea Estates (India) Limited, in the Coonoor Club and had asked him if he could suggest a suitable candidate. It was a daring move as until then there was no Indian Executive in SITE. Madden was always the first to do this or the first to do that, and he had made up his mind to prove to the others who were still sitting on the fence that an Indian in their set-up would actually fit in. There was also a letter from Madden to my uncle detailing the terms of employment. When I saw the terms, I baulked. The pay that was being offered, including dearness allowance, was two hundred rupees less than what I was drawing in the Army as a junior Captain. The rupee in those days was a strong currency. A tin of fifty Capstan Navy Cut cigarettes (that I smoked) cost just three rupees, and a bottle of Scotch whisky, twenty five rupees in the open market. I declined to attend the interview. My uncle wrote again telling me that I should not be put off by the salary offered as there would be other benefits like an annual bonus to boost my income and urged me to come down to Cochin for the interview.

I allowed myself to be persuaded, and duly arrived in Cochin.

When I met Madden for the interview, I was completely self-assured. Three years of commissioned service in the Army during which time I had met all kinds of men had prepared me mentally for anything that life was going to throw at me. Madden, a big-made man, was dressed in a pair of blue corduroy shorts and a short-sleeved shirt. He had a questionnaire in front of him – two foolscap pages full of queries. There was practically nothing that he didn't want to know about me. For the life of me, I couldn't think why my brothers' names, complete with their initials, and what they did for a living, and other similarly inconsequential questions, had to be satisfactorily answered for me to qualify for the job on offer. My youngest brother has an initial H to his name and I pronounced the letter as 'haitch', emphasizing the 'h'. Madden couldn't let it pass and said, "Your 'aitches' are not too good, are they?" Suddenly, and in the middle of his inexorable inquisition, he asked me where I was staying in Cochin. The only hotel I had heard of in Cochin was the Malabar Hotel, so I had booked myself a room in that establishment. When Madden learned I was staying at the Malabar Hotel, he looked pleased and said, "Good for you." I discovered later that all the British planters and their families always stayed at the Malabar when they came down from the estates on leave, or when passing through. I knew I had made a favourable impression.

Two days later when I was still in Madras with my family, I received a telegram from Madden to say that the Company's Board in London had approved of my appointment as an Assistant Superintendent in his Company. He had sent them a cable soon after he had interviewed me, and had received their reply immediately afterwards.

I was due to fulfil yet another long-cherished wish of mine. I was about to become a tea planter.

When I applied for my release from the Army, Khush Bakht Singh Bhinder (the same brother officer who visited me on the estates several years after I'd left the Army), was in the Army Headquarters. He helped to push my papers along and, as a result, I managed to get out of the Army in fairly quick time. Into the bargain, I also managed to beat the deadline that Madden had set for me to join his Company. Madden's seeming haste to get me installed in SITE without delay was understandable. He was shortly due to leave on furlough for six months, so he was keen that I sign the agreement with the Company before he left.

Three estates – Glenmary, Ladrum and Kuduakarnam – comprised SITE. Each of them was further sub-divided into divisions. I was first posted to Glenmary Estate. I arrived there at nightfall on Friday, 10 April 1953, a date that I shall remember all my life. I was met by a man called Douglas Richardson who was to be my Superintendent. As was the custom, after I reported for duty, I stayed with him and his wife for three nights before moving into my own small bungalow. On Sunday, while the three of us were sitting on the verandah after breakfast, Oswald William Horrocks (Ossie to all who knew him, and they were legion) arrived. Horrocks was the Superintendent of Ladrum Estate, the best estate in the Company. Horrocks sported a huge RAF-type handlebar moustache, and I wondered if he was as fierce as he looked. If ever looks belied a man, his did. I discovered later that he had one of the gentlest hearts that ever ticked inside a human breast.

My bungalow was perched on top of a hill, not too far from the General Manager's bungalow and directly in line with it. The first occupant of the bungalow, for whom it was built, was Horrocks. When I mentioned to Horrocks sometime after I occupied the bungalow that it had a magnificent hibiscus hedge in front, he said he had raised it. And for a sound purpose. According to Horrocks, he hadn't been in the bungalow very long before he discovered that he was under the surveillance of his General Manager, a man called JS Wilkie, a tartar. Apparently, Wilkie would train his binoculars periodically on Horrocks' bungalow to keep an eye on him. Literally. Horrocks was a simple man but he was damned if he was going to give the General Manager the pleasure of spying on him for much longer. He got a deep trench dug in front of his bungalow, filled it with cowdung and other stuff, and put down hibiscus cuttings. The hibiscus cuttings took root rapidly, and within a short time, Wilkie could not watch Horrocks from his drawing room window any more. When I occupied the bungalow thirty years later, the hibiscus plants continued to be in very good health.

After he had established his hibiscus hedge and felt safe from the prying eyes of his General Manager, Horrocks found that a cow had started visiting his garden every evening to feed on the lush grass that grew there. He went to Wilkie and complained about the nuisance and sought his advice on how to deal with the problem. Wilkie gave him his shotgun and a couple of cartridges to 'frighten' off the cow. The next evening, when the cow came for her usual evening meal, Horrocks loaded the gun as instructed, and proceeded towards the cow which was not perturbed as she had seen him before. Horrocks walked up to the cow, put the gun against her side and pulled the trigger. The result was dramatic. The cow keeled over and died.

Horrocks couldn't understand, of course, why the owner of the cow and his friends came up to the bungalow and created such a ruckus. He didn't know any Tamil, and couldn't follow a word of what they were shouting. The labourers then went to Wilkie and complained about Horrocks. The matter was eventually settled when the owner of the cow was compensated for his loss, and Horrocks knew some peace thereafter.

The bungalow I lived in was compact and comfortable. Even if it was small compared to the bungalows occupied by the Superintendents, it was palatial when set against the small Army tent (in which you could only stand upright in the middle) that I had lived in for two years before I joined the Company. I had a large bedroom all to myself with a comfortable bed, and the luxury of an attached bathroom. The furniture that the bungalow had was rather more than what Horrocks had been given when he went to live in it in 1923. He was told then that it was considered adequate for a bachelor, and it was the barest minimum possible.

There was no electricity in the house, and I was expected to make my own lighting arrangements. I had one petromax lantern for the sitting room, and a number of oil lamps lit up the other rooms when needed. There were no diversions of any kind, not even a radio, but since I was fond of reading, I really couldn't complain. I became a member of a book club in Bombay, and every month they would send me a catalogue from which I had to buy at least one book. A hardback in those days cost less than ten rupees. I also became a member of a library in Madras, and the books that I chose to read were sent to me by post. The Peermade Club too, of which I became a member, had an interesting collection of books in its library, and since I also subscribed to various magazines, there was no dearth of reading matter.

The bungalow had a tin roof just a few feet above my head. The South-West monsoon, for which Travancore was famous, started barely two months after I moved in. And the rain came down in torrents. The constant drumming of the heavy rain on the tin roof just above my head was very unnerving. After all, I grew up in Trichinopoly (famous for its cigars which Winston Churchill was said to have smoked), and lived in North India during my service in the Army – places where it hardly ever rained.

My Superintendent, Douglas Richardson, was the only son of JA Richardson – known simply as JAR to all. JAR was a Ceylon planter, as a number of early planters in the Peermade-Vandiperiyar district were. He was engaged in planting in the High Range in Travancore before he moved to Peermade in 1905 where he became the General Manager of my Company, a post he held for several years. He was a powerful figure as a planter. He was elected to the Legislative Council in Trivandrum in 1910, and was also a member of the Madras Legislative Council from 1919 to 1922. He was elected Chairman of UPASI for the years 1909 and 1914. At his initiative, the South Indian Association was formed in London. To my knowledge, it continued to function for a long time, and many retired planters from South India met each year to renew their old friendships at its annual reunion. JAR strode the planting scene in South India like a colossus at the turn of the twentieth century. Apart from his achievements as a planter, he was strikingly handsome (from the photograph I saw of him), and he seemed to be fully conscious of his good looks and personality. In contrast, his son, Douglas, in spite of the private wealth he was reported to have possessed (certainly far more than his contemporaries did), was a modest man who lived and dreamt tea.

I must digress here a little to relate an incident which affected me somewhat at the time it happened. One of the main reasons why anyone chose to join and serve in a foreign Company in those distant days was because the emoluments were better than in an Indian Company.

A prominent South Indian plantations Company had as its chief an Indian Christian like me, and he was greatly respected by members of the Christian community in South India. He had worked as a clerk under JAR in the very Company that I later joined. He was a clever man, a man of enterprise and foresight, who recognized the opportunity planting offered to become rich and famous. By dint of hard work and with the kind of luck one has to have as a pioneer, he acquired a number of estates, both tea and rubber, and put them all together to form, in due course, a formidable empire.

My uncle, Pandiaraj Davidar, worked as a senior Manager in one of the Companies owned by this man. By the time I had become a planter, Uncle Pandiaraj had been transferred from The Nilgiris to Arnakal Estate in Central Travancore, a large estate fairly close to my own, one of the three tea estates in the two Companies his boss owned in my district. As the Chairman and Managing Director of his Companies, my uncle's boss was looking for a Visiting Agent. Visiting Agents were usually outsiders who had to periodically visit the estates and report on them for a fee. This wealthy man admired *all* Englishmen. Madden was both available and willing to be his Visiting Agent. He got the job.

When Madden went on his first visit to Arnakal Estate, the boss man was there in person to greet him. The man had with him a senior employee of his Company, a sidekick who was nearly always present, and my uncle. In their presence, he asked Madden, without much ado, what my pay was going to be.

This question was asked not without malice aforethought. Madden had been in India for far too long to be naïve about why the query was put to him. Suppressing the dearness allowance component of my pay, he replied, "Two hundred and fifty rupees." The man had the audacity to say, "That's right, don't pay him more." (His actual words, as told to me by my uncle.) This man was not paying me his money. Nor did he have to teach Madden how to keep his Indian employees economically subservient. The Gujaratis have an apt saying to describe such unwarranted declarations. '*Tara baap noo soo jayech*', translated literally means, 'How does it affect your father?' More simply, it is used to remark dismissively, "How does it concern you?"

I learnt later that his own Executive Staff received poor salaries, so my uncle's boss was probably attempting to cover his own behind by suggesting to Madden what I should be paid. This conversation had obviously been leaked, as a junior man in his Company whom I got to know later said to me one day that I wasn't being paid all that much after all, was I?

The man's attitude reminded me of one of the characteristics for which the Indian crab is reputed. A stranger to the business was aghast that Indian crabs for sale were transported in open crates. He enquired whether the crabs would reach their destination safely. He was told that any crab trying to make good its escape by climbing up the side of the open crate would be promptly pulled down by the others. My uncle's boss personified the Indian crab.

After all, I did not grudge the man his stupendous success in life, nor his son – whom I knew in college – his playboy lifestyle as he drove around Madras in the evenings in his large and gleaming Armstrong-Siddelly sports car with the hood down while I pedalled my bicycle, my regular transport.

One evening after work, sometime after I had joined, I was in the estate factory overseeing some manufacturing process when I was told that the Head Tea Maker of another estate in the Company was outside and wished to see me. A rather frail-looking man greeted me when I went out. He seemed genuinely pleased to meet me. He said he would be retiring from the Company's service very shortly and wanted to see me before he left. He volunteered the information that he and the wealthy man – mentioned earlier – were cousins. They had both started out in life here in the same Company. "He in the office, and I in the factory. I am still here, and he is rounding the world (sic)," he concluded. He said all this without the slightest trace of rancour. His transport was a bullock cart which he owned, and he was not ashamed of it. Unlike his cousin, he wished me well before he left.

∿

Early Days

My work for the first few months was entirely in the field. This consisted of supervising the women who were engaged to pluck tea leaves (pluckers); and the men whose work was chiefly weeding the fields manually, spraying or dusting pesticides and maintaining the roads. When the General Manager got me to sign the standard agreement in his office, he had dressed for the occasion in a freshly-laundered white shirt and khaki shorts, and wore a red polka-dotted bow tie. He told me then that if I had anything to do with the pluckers, it would be twenty fours' notice for me. He said this without batting an eyelid, looking me straight in the eye which bespoke brazenness, as he himself had been known to be quite a lad when he first came out to India as a teenager to become a planter. It was quite acceptable in those days for the young men to seek out local women. Richardson, my Superintendent, the only other person in the room, had obviously told the other planters of Madden's warning to me, because the senior planters, when I came to know them well, never failed to pull my leg unmercifully about it. I felt, in retrospect, that Madden could have been a little tactful and told me that it would be dangerous in the conditions that prevailed to have anything to do with the women pluckers.

It didn't take superior intellect to know that with changing times, playing around with the women on the estate could lead to a highly explosive state of affairs. India had become independent, trade unions had proliferated, and the leaders of the labour unions were always looking for weaknesses to exploit. One man told me seriously that after Independence, the planters who had the most labour trouble were the ones who had played around the most with the women on their estates. Some of them, though, did not just 'love 'em and leave 'em'. I used to play tennis and cricket in Peermade and usually bought my sporting equipment from the Pioneer Sports Company on Mount Road in Madras. On one such occasion, a light-skinned salesman attended on me. He spoke English with a pronounced South Indian accent. When I asked him if I could pay for my purchases by cheque he agreed, but asked me for my address. When I wrote it down, he looked at it and asked if I worked in Peermade. When I answered in the affirmative, he asked if I knew Bon Ami estate. "Yes," I said again. He then asked if I knew one Chaarlus Patterson (sic). I replied in the negative. He then went on to say that this man, Patterson, used to send his mother, who was Indian, some money regularly each month, but it had stopped coming sometime earlier. At that point, we parted company. Time passed on, and when Horrocks became my Superintendent, I mentioned this conversation to him. Horrocks said Patterson had died, which explained why the remittances had stopped.

In actual fact, Madden needn't have worried. Apart from common sense, the main division of Glenmary Estate, of which I was put in charge, comprised about five hundred and thirty acres – almost as extensive as some medium-sized estates were. Walking up and down the hills – and some were steep – as I did to visit every single work spot, made me invariably feel so tired by the end of the evening that I usually dropped off the moment my head hit the pillow at night. Slumber was never so deep and dreamless. Where then, was the question of having anything to do with the wenches?

After about a couple of months of foot-slogging, I acquired my first motorcycle. Willie, my younger brother in Madras, had a second-hand BSA motorcycle (called the 'Beeza') which my father had bought for him. He decided, graciously, that it would be more useful for me on the estate than for him in

Madras, and sent it to me by lorry transport. I thoroughly enjoyed riding the bike around the division. Richardson had no objection, and encouraged the idea in fact. On occasion, he would lead me on his bike – a Triumph, I think, a heavy one. He was an excellent rider. I remember the Plucking Writer once telling me that Richardson could take his bike up hills where only a goat could go. Richardson was also a superb mechanic, something I could never aspire to become. He repaired my bike for me on a couple of occasions when it broke down.

Madden returned after six months of furlough in England. Almost the first thing he did was to order me to stop riding around the estate. He didn't do it directly himself, but got Richardson to tell me that during the morning hours I should walk around the division. As my day started in the field at 7.30 am and lasted till 1 pm when I went home for lunch, I was on my feet for several hours each day. In the afternoons, I couldn't ride my motorcycle much because the men had left after doing their allotted tasks, and only the pluckers were at work. Not only did Madden stop me from riding the motorcycle, once when he saw me walking on the road going from one field to another, he told me that I should take short cuts through the fields, as the English have a saying, 'A farmer's boots are the best manure'. By this time, much as I liked working outdoors and the clean fresh air, I was getting quite fed up with the daily routine with no chance of using any kind of brain power. Col Spain was right. There was indeed no glamour in planting.

I had a lot of spare time at my disposal when I was not actually trudging around, so I thought I would develop my interest in writing. In the magazine, *The Illustrated Weekly of India*, to which I subscribed, a correspondence course in short story writing was advertised. I wrote to the institute in Bombay which ran the course, and they asked me to write a short story and send it to them to assess my ability to write. Horrocks was once showing off to his friends in my presence his ability to speak in Tamil. He quoted a Tamil proverb, *'Ikkaraiku akkarai pachai irukku'*, which when translated literally means, 'To this side (of the river), the other side greener is'. I couldn't have asked for a better theme. Naturally, the title of my story was *The Other Side of the River*. It was autobiographical. When the hero of the story was in the Army, life as a planter had seemed to him most attractive. When he actually did become a planter, and was one for only a few months, he realized that life in the Army in spite of its dull, peacetime routine in a field area, was actually more tolerable. I used some dialogue in the story, and sent off my finished work. When the institute wrote back, they opined my story was amateurish and picked other holes in it. In their final analysis, they felt I had some potential as a writer, and were confident that with their expert coaching, I could become a reasonably good one. The colour of my money was what interested them. I registered myself for the course. The first lessons were elementary, and after a few lessons which seemed to lead nowhere, I gave up. My dream of becoming a writer died with it.

At about this time, there was also a course called Pelmanism which was being offered by another magazine. I remember the advertisement said that if you had a grasshopper mind, they'd change it for you. How did the mind of a grasshopper work, how did *they* know how it worked? Horrocks (who will increasingly appear in my story) said to me once he didn't know what he really wanted to do and thought a course in Pelmanism might help. He enrolled in a correspondence course, and at the end of each lesson, he was asked what his object in life was. Horrocks didn't know what his object in life was, so he gave up the course.

In its natural state, tea is a tree. As in so many other instances, the practice of pruning was a chance discovery according to Alan Mcfarlane, the son of an Assam tea planter, in his excellent and unbiased book, *Green Gold: The Empire of Tea*, a book anybody interested in tea would benefit by reading, co-authored with his mother Iris Mcfarlane, a tea planter's widow. He says that the villagers in Assam cut down the tea trees in the fields that were being prepared for cultivating rice. Two months later when harvesting the paddy, they found that the stumps had sprouted. When allowed to grow, the tea trees attained a height of ten feet. Charles Bruce, the brother of Robert Bruce who is believed to have first discovered the tea plant in Assam, apparently pruned the ten-foot trees back to four feet, and found shoots sprouting below the cut. Mcfarlane writes that the first lesson learnt in tea cultivation was that tea grew faster when pruned. After that, it was only a matter of experimenting with the optimum pruning height to maximize commercial exploitation.

When I joined SITE in 1953, I saw some trees dotted about in a field of healthy tea. When I asked about them, I was told they were tea trees and were known as seed bearers. Some vigorous tea bushes were allowed to grow into trees and seeds were collected from them. The seedlings that were raised from those seeds were put out in the existing fields to fill up vacancies or to develop new fields. That same year, the seed bearers were cut down to the level of the other tea bushes and remained as such because my Company had started cultivating tea plants from leaf or internodal cuttings called clonal cuttings. The plants that grew from the clonal cuttings were favoured because they assumed the same characteristics of the plants from which the cuttings were chosen, whereas the quality of the tea plants that grew from seeds formed from cross-pollinated flowers was unpredictable. Ceylon (now Sri Lanka) was at the forefront in this field of endeavour. Several of the tea clones from that country were grown in the estates in Southern India, including our own with excellent results because Peermade resembled Ceylon in many respects.

In our Company, a field was normally pruned once in four years. When the new flush appeared and the fresh stalks attained a certain maturity, they were snipped or 'tipped' to the height at which the plucking table was to be maintained. One afternoon I went to a plucking field where the tipping gang was in action. The tipping gang was the elite plucking gang in any division. When this field was about to be tipped, the Plucking Writer asked me which pluckers should be selected for the tipping gang. It was a bait. I rose to it. I answered, "The best." Some of the best pluckers were middle-aged women, and not exactly good-looking. When I got to the field, Madden was already there. He occupied the General Manager's bungalow which was on my division and not too far from my own. That day, Madden was walking up and down the cycle path that ran through the field. The pluckers were spread out both above and below the path. He didn't seem to be in the best of tempers. When he saw me, Madden said without preamble, "Oh, Davidar, it is usual to have young girls in the tipping gang because – he hesitated, obviously groping for the right words – because they are accurate." He had come to check out the young girls on the division where he lived, and was disappointed with what he saw. He never came to my tipping gang again.

Madden's counterpart in the other British Company in the district was more honest. He had taken a liking to me, and he once told me that when he came out to India as a young man in the 1920s, a few years after Madden, the pluckers didn't wear blouses. If one was curious to see what was *choli ke peeche*, all one had to do was to part the saree a little and take a peek. No offence was taken. In those days, a planter was free to do just about anything without any opposition from anybody, most notably the labour unions that were non-existent before the country became independent. The men who came out from England and Scotland to plant were in their teens. With the lonesomeness becoming oppressive and fire raging in their loins, female companionship when sought was not frowned upon. It was almost deemed a necessity. Again, as Alan Mcfarlane says in his admirable book, *Green Gold: The Empire of Tea,* a young Englishman may not have been well paid but he enjoyed a lifestyle that not too many would have known at Home – a house with many servants, and women brought to his bed whenever needed, whose services were paid for with bars of soap.

I was always running into Madden as he rode around on his motorcycle. One afternoon he called me to his office which was close to his bungalow, and adjacent to my own estate office. He questioned me closely to find out how much I had learned about tea planting when he was away on furlough. There was no love lost between Richardson and Madden. Although I had done all that I was required to do, Madden stated solemnly at the end of the interview that I had been wasting my time. He also said that from then on he would educate me. I must have been a good pupil because he told me after a short time that I had made very good progress.

One day he asked me if I knew how to use a tracer and pole. When I professed ignorance, he said he'd teach me. He asked me to arrange for a tracer and pole to be sent up to his bungalow, and invited me to tea the following evening, after which my lesson would start. He taught me how to use the two simple instruments to trace a road at the required gradient. It was easy and he complimented me on how quick I was on the uptake. I should have known there was a catch in it somewhere. There was. Madden said I should put into practice what I had learnt. For a start, he told me to trace a cycle path from his gate straight up to his bungalow. A perfectly good tarred road was already there, but it had a hairpin bend about twenty yards from the bungalow which he wanted to avoid. Next, he asked me to trace a path with two U-bends in the new vegetable garden that Mrs Madden wanted to raise behind their bungalow, which I did. The vegetable garden was a great success. Mrs Madden told me that she never bought any vegetables, and always grew her own. And they were very good ones too. She was the exact opposite of her husband.

While she was a friendly type and down-to-earth, he was pompous.

In course of time, Madden and I became good friends as we were probably the only men in the Company who read books in our spare time. He would occasionally borrow the odd book that I was buying from the Universal Book Club in Bombay. I particularly enjoyed real-life adventure books like Thor Heyerdahl's *Kon-Tiki Expedition*, and he appeared to have a similar taste in reading.

When Madden learnt that I also read the *Time* magazine (a habit that began in my college days), he offered to lend me his copy after he had gone through it. With uncanny foresight, he had availed himself of the introductory offer made by *Time* for the supply of the magazine for one's lifetime for a one-time down payment when the magazine was first launched. It saved me some money as I could stop my own subscription. Reading that magazine, which I did from cover to cover, was pure joy.

Sixteen years after I was employed in SITE, I was elevated to the No.1 position in the Company, contrary to expectations in some quarters. On the eve of my ascending the 'gaddi', Madden, who had been a Director of the Company for some ten years, wrote to congratulate me. He said, "I think you owe your success to *Time*, and I think you should make your young men in due course to buy it and read it. I say this in all seriousness."

Madden didn't know the men I commanded. Except for one man, I doubt that any of the others read any book, or anything for that matter. But they were happy and had all come to stay. Francis Bacon, the eminent essayist, wrote, 'Reading maketh a full man'. But, a full man in that sense may not necessarily have made a happy tea planter.

∽

Of Geese and General Managers

Madden figured prominently in the last few months I was on Glenmary division. I would meet him practically every day somewhere or the other. He believed in being a trailblazer. He had to be the first in everything. He boasted he was the first to install an English bath in a Superintendent's bungalow, the first to lay a strip of concrete in front of his bungalow (which was still there after fifty years), the first to introduce vegetative propagation of tea in the district, the first to engage an Indian Executive in a British Company in the district.....the list went on and on. There was a crime fiction writer by the name of Peter Cheyney whose books I loved to read in my early youth. The one recurring theme in his novels was, 'Try anything once'. I don't know if Madden had read any of his books, but he'd try anything, just about anything.

Since Madden and I shared a passion for reading, he'd tell me about some book or article that he had read recently whenever he ran into me in the field. One day he mentioned a very interesting article he had just read in the *Reader's Digest*. The article he said could have some application in tea. I should have heard the alarm bells clanging but didn't.

It was all about a farmer in the Philippines who had successfully used geese to weed his paddy fields. Now, weeds were a serious problem in the tea fields. It was tedious work to do a reasonably good job of weeding, both for the worker who pretended to remove them and for the Supervisor whose unenviable job it was to get it done. Madden rightly called the job of weeding unproductive labour, and was always looking for ways and means of getting the weeds eliminated in the tea fields, simply and effectively.

Madden decided that if a farmer in the Philippines could use geese to get rid of the weeds in his paddy fields, he, Madden, would use them to sort out the weeds in his tea fields. Madden announced, and I should have expected it, that I, as the dogsbody, was going to carry out the experiment for him.

I was instructed to have an enclosure erected with *eetta*, a thin, reedy kind of bamboo which grew wild in the vicinity of the estate. Typically, *eetta* was used to weave the baskets that the pluckers slung on their backs to catch the tea leaves that they picked and deftly chucked over their shoulders. The enclosure was to be in a convenient spot, close to the road, where the geese would be kept and observed. The enclosure was soon ready, and a goose and a gander were ceremoniously released into it. The experiment that was going to revolutionize weeding in tea had begun.

The arrival of the birds unfortunately coincided with the onset of the dry weather, and there were precious few weeds anyhow. The geese were more interested in getting out of the enclosure than in tackling any weeds. As the enclosure was fairly close to my bungalow, I would stand and watch the geese every time I went to work and returned. It was a good way to kill time. The geese would walk round and round, then come to where I was standing and look at me reproachfully. The geese and I were bored to tears. Madden would join me now and then, and we would both stand and watch the perambulating geese in companionable silence. He enquired anxiously one day if the geese were doing their stuff. Of course, they weren't. Eventually, he came to the reluctant conclusion that our geese were not as committed as the ones that the farmer in the Philippines had. One day he asked me if I knew what happened to the eggs that the goose should have been laying. It hadn't crossed my mind, so I didn't have an answer. Madden was of the firm opinion that the senior staff member who was entrusted with the job of looking after the geese at night was helping himself to the eggs. But the man stoutly denied all knowledge when I asked him about it.

The experiment was deemed inconclusive and discontinued. Who likes to admit defeat anyhow? The geese were shifted to the General Manager's bungalow, and I was transferred shortly afterwards to another estate, so I never found out what happened to them.

Madden wasn't going to give up even if the geese didn't cooperate. If you thought of tenacity of purpose, you would think of Madden. He had been quietly casting about for alternate methods of weed control when the geese let him down. He had heard somewhere that fire would fix the weeds. He had discovered that a neighbouring estate had a portable flame-thrower – why they kept one, God alone knows. He promptly arranged to borrow it. I was still around, and was, therefore, a great asset. I was to handle the machine, and was given instructions on how to operate it. The fateful experiment was to be carried out in a plot of China tea bushes (which are very low to the ground) that was near the estate factory and close to the General Manager's bungalow. When the appointed time arrived, and with Madden watching from the road, I went to work. It didn't occur to me to find out where my Superintendent, Richardson, was when all these experiments were being carried out on the main division of his estate. I think he didn't want to get mixed up in any hare-brained scheme, and quite sensibly, kept away. Anyway, the flame-thrower worked beautifully, and the weeds were completely scorched. But the tea bushes also got badly burned. Yet another project that seemed to be pregnant with possibility had to be prematurely abandoned.

For the record, Madden scored yet another 'first' in the district. A few years after he retired to England and joined the Company's Board as a Director, he arranged with Imperial Chemical Industries (ICI), the biggest chemical industries company in England, to send their representatives to the Company's estates in Peermade to demonstrate the efficacy of their wonder weedicide, *Gramoxone*, that they had recently developed. Madden was also visiting the estates at the time, but it was not a coincidence. The picture of a beaming Madden standing in the field surrounded by all the Company's Executives while the two men deputed by ICI from England sprayed the weedicide for our benefit remains indelibly etched in my mind to this day. He had indeed started a revolution. Madden never gave up.

When Madden came on his next visit after introducing us to *Gramoxone*, I was the Superintendent of Ladrum Estate. I had constructed a small dam close to the estate nursery, on the grounds that we would have water for the nursery plants close by, a prime requirement. I also planned to develop the area around the dam as a park, and put down some shrubs which started to come on nicely. The staff on the division also became enthusiastic about the project and got involved. One of them brought some water lily plants which I introduced into the dam, and they began to thrive. When Madden came around to the nursery, the water lily plants were flowering profusely. The whole effect was like a painting by Monet. I pointed out the water lilies in full bloom to Madden with some pride. Shaking his head from side to side he said, "*Gramoxone*, Davidar, *Gramoxone*."

I mentioned this incident to my General Manager who had obviously spread the story abroad. Sometime later, I met the No.1 of TTE in the Club, a close friend of Madden's. He asked me with a mischievous smile on his face, "How are your water lilies doing, Davidar?"

One morning, during the first year of my service in the Company as an Assistant on Glenmary division, Richardson and I were in the field when Madden came and joined us. While they discussed something that had to be done, I stood around on 'listening watch'. Suddenly, Madden said to

Richardson, pointing to me, "You know, Richardson, this chap here has an advantage over the rest of us. He's a Botany BSc, you know." I was acutely embarrassed. The early planters who came out from Britain were barely out of school, and were usually in their teens. At this point, I think it is necessary to narrate how I came to be a Botany BSc.

English was my favourite subject both in school and in college. I did well in English at the intermediate level – the minimum period of two years of study before one could go on to do a degree. Naturally, I chose to major in English for my degree as well. I applied for the three-year, BA (Honours) English Literature course and was given admission. In the first year, Old English was one of the subjects we had to study. It was like learning a new language. As it was considered a most difficult subject, one or two chaps in the second year told me that in order to get promoted, I had to do well in Old English. They also said that the other subjects didn't matter too much as I could always make up in them as I went along. For some reason, languages came rather easily to me, and I did very well in Old English in the final exam. I was detained though. When I sent for the marks to know what had gone wrong, I found that in both English prose and in English poetry, I had fallen short of passing by just two or three marks in each subject. Now, these subjects are not like Mathematics or Physics in which the answers have to be accurate in order to score the required pass-marks. One didn't fail in English prose and poetry by just a couple of marks; and even if that was possible, in all likelihood, a few marks would be added to see one through. I felt that it was grossly unfair. I couldn't think how I could have offended the two lecturers in question.

Quite convinced that an injustice had been done to me, I decided to appeal to the highest authority in the college. I wrote to the Principal of the college, a Scotsman, the Reverend Alexander John Boyd (he was later conferred the richly-deserved degree of Doctor of Divinity). In my considered opinion, and that of the others who knew him, there was no better college Principal either before him or since. He was a most remarkable man. He took part in every activity of the college and lived for it. After college hours, he put on his khaki shorts and visited every playing field, cheerily greeting whomsoever he met. What was most extraordinary about him was his ability to address every student by name. And, there were more than a thousand students in the college, both resident and non-resident. If a student had been in the college for a couple of years, he would know his name; if the student continued in the college for a further length of time, he would call him by his first name. How he achieved this feat, nobody ever found out.

A few days after I wrote to him, there was a reply from the great man himself. He addressed me as 'My dear Eddie'. He fully sympathized with me over my misfortune, then went on to say that he didn't like to interfere with the decisions taken in the matter of promotions by the Heads of Departments. Further, he made me the magnanimous offer that should I wish to continue with my studies in his college, I could ask him for *any* degree course, and he would grant me admission to it. How could I argue with the man after such a conciliatory letter? I considered my options for a few days. I liked plants generally, and more importantly, as Botany seemed to be one of the easier courses on offer, I decided to major in it and asked the Principal for a seat. My admission card arrived promptly.

Richardson was obviously not amused by Madden's remark. On one or two occasions, after telling me what needed to be done in the field, he would exclaim, "What would Botany BSc say to that?" In actual fact, the Botany I studied in the classroom was of very little use in tea planting. I would simply say to Richardson that I'd arrange to get things done the way he wished. Obviously mollified by my humble approach, he forgave me for being a Botany BSc. He never ever taunted me again.

∾

Ghosts, Snakes and Labour Trouble

Of the eight divisions in the Company, Ranikoil had earned the reputation of being the most notorious because the labour on the division was the most troublesome. I was transferred to Ranikoil after I had been on Glenmary division for almost a year. I got to Ranikoil at the beginning of March, and the afternoon rains arrived right on schedule towards the end of the month. We had applied to our tea, at the right time, a much-touted artificial manure which had produced the most beneficial results in Ceylon (now Sri Lanka). The tea responded as never before. In a month's time, we had the most phenomenal rush of crop and we could hardly cope. The pluckers were in the fields at daybreak and carried on till nightfall. The more crop they plucked, the higher their wages. The men were also allowed to pluck in the afternoons after they had finished their regular work, and they passed on what they plucked to their wives or relatives. Further, luck was also on our side. Our bountiful harvest coincided with a shortage of tea in the other tea-producing countries, and the law of supply and demand worked in our favour. The quality of our teas was mostly indifferent, but the prices they fetched were unheard of. Everybody was happy and the Company made a huge profit.

The ban on my riding the motorcycle while at work continued to remain in force. I did not mind as walking around helped to pass the time. Ranikoil division was four miles long and about one hundred yards wide – the area occupied by tea was about three miles long. Just one lorry road ran through the division from top to bottom, almost right in the middle of the tea.

All went well for a time. As I was a newcomer whose strengths and weaknesses had yet to be assessed, the workers allowed themselves to be told what to do. But it was not in their nature to take things lying down indefinitely. Some of the ringleaders, encouraged by the labour union leaders who loved to fish in troubled waters, started playing up, imperceptibly at first, and overtly as time went by. Orders by the staff were questioned, and on every conceivable occasion, the labour would resort to go-slow tactics. It was something that one could not effectively control since the Government of the day tended to go soft on labour. The men worked tardily, so the weeds proliferated and got out of hand; the pluckers fearing the wrath of the militant menfolk, went about plucking at a leisurely pace. The staff were threatened with violence. All the bonhomie of a few months earlier had dissipated. Even my orders meant for nothing. As a Tamil, I had frequent slanging matches with the rowdy elements. There was much indiscipline on the division, and the crop started falling. As the General Manager, Madden got worried. He sent for Horrocks, the Superintendent of Ladrum Estate (of which Ranikoil was a part) and me, the Assistant Superintendent, to discuss the problem. Horrocks said to Madden that I was at a disadvantage because I spoke the language of the labour and tended to retaliate when they were rude, whereas they, the British, could always pretend that they didn't understand what the workers were saying. The conference ended with no solution to the problem. Like any fever, the trouble had to run its course.

One outcome of the meeting was encouraging, however. It was decided that I should be vested with disciplinary powers, and the Superintendent had to issue a notice to that effect. I could charge-sheet erring workers who, if found guilty, would be punished in accordance with the rules in force. It was the first time that an Assistant Superintendent was given such authority. Drastic situations, obviously, demanded drastic solutions.

When I joined the Company, there was no uniform procedure to charge-sheet workers and conduct enquiries on the estates. During my first year, Madden told me one day that the Indian Army had a standard procedure for conducting Courts of Enquiry. He asked if I could procure the form that was used for this purpose in the Army. I wrote to my friend in the Army Headquarters, Khush Bakht Singh Bhinder, and asked if he would oblige. And, oblige he did. He promptly sent me the form which I passed on to Madden. Madden revised the form to meet the requirements of the estates, then sent it to the Secretary of the State Planters' Association, suggesting that it be formally approved as the procedure to be followed uniformly by all the estates belonging to the Association. It was accepted, and thereafter, the form that Madden put forward to conduct a domestic enquiry was adopted by all the estates of the Association.

Even with stricter procedures in place, the power struggle between the management and the labour continued regardless. Each tried to dominate the other. One evening I was walking back to my bungalow in a filthy temper, as minutes before I had been bested in a nasty argument with the union leaders on the division. By the side of the road, I saw the rear of a snake hanging out of a hole in a tall bank. Ranikoil was situated at an elevation of about three thousand five hundred feet above sea level, which was lower than any other division in the Company. Consequently, cobras abounded in that one division alone. Without thinking, I caught the snake by its tail and gradually eased it out. When I'd pulled it out completely, I swung it in the air and brought it down with full force, head first, like an intrepid uncle of mine was known to have done to the cobras in Trichinopoly. It died instantly. Unfortunately, it turned out to be a rat snake which would have actually been useful to keep down the rat population. If I had realized it before, I wouldn't have harmed the rat snake. But I was committed to killing it, and couldn't stop to check whether it was a rat snake or a cobra. I had a vague feeling that someone was watching me, so I turned round to look. A male worker was standing a few paces behind me, his eyes wide with fear. He may have related this incident to the others as I didn't have any trouble with the workers for some time afterwards. It was too good to last though.

If I was not going to be spared, the staff on the division fared much worse. The main target of the labour was the Conductor, the chief among the field staff, whose job it was, among others, to allot work to the men every day. One day, he decided that he'd had enough, and planned to teach the baddies a lesson in his own way. The estate factory, located on the main division of Ladrum Estate, was separated from Ranikoil by a strip of Indian-owned, proprietary estate, and the road between them also ran through it. The Conductor had quietly liaised with some tough guys on the private estate, who were employed by that management for the express purpose of keeping their labour in line, to deal with the rowdies on Ranikoil. He then sent the troublemakers to the factory on a prearranged day.

The Conductor didn't tell me what he had surreptitiously arranged. That day, he left for his house immediately after the morning muster. Just as I was finishing breakfast, I heard a terrible commotion outside. When I looked out of the dining room window, I saw a number of men yelling and screaming. I went out to investigate, and saw one of the leading rowdies on the division bleeding from the head, and his eyes were red. A couple of his pals were also injured, though not bleeding like their friend. They shouted that they wanted an instant decision. They had rushed to the Conductor's house to confront him, as they knew instinctively that he was responsible for their plight. They were right, of course. The Conductor had arranged with the toughs on the neighbouring estate to beat up these chaps on their way to the estate factory. He knew what would happen, so he had hurried home, bolted all the doors and windows, and wisely stayed inside. As they couldn't get hold of him, the men who were roughed up made a beeline for my bungalow.

I couldn't think of what to say. The men were understandably very angry. I told them to come to the division office where I would talk to them. The situation was decidedly ugly. I jumped on my motorcycle, and raced to the office to await the mob. And, to think of a plan of action. The rabble duly arrived, and they wanted to know what I was going to do. They demanded justice. I told them to be quiet, and asked one of them to tell me what had actually happened. But, would they listen?

Just then, a stroke of luck came my way. The road that led from the labour lines to the fields below ran just in front of the office. As the pluckers were setting out from their homes, a couple of chaps were holding them up, and I heard one of them say that nobody would be allowed to go to work unless I took proper action. This good fortune was unexpected. I warned the rowdies that if anyone was prevented from going to work, I would do nothing. The result was more than I imagined possible. The same chaps who were forcibly stopping the pluckers, now quietly asked them to go on their way. After that, the situation became somewhat manageable.

I told the men that I was sorry that they were beaten up so badly, but this was a case of assault and battery in which some outsiders were involved, so I could do nothing myself. But I promised that I would go to the estate office and ask the Superintendent to immediately prefer a complaint with the Police, and urge them to take the necessary action promptly. Beyond my expectation, they calmed down. Heaving a tremendous sigh of relief, I rode to the estate office and told Horrocks all that had happened. He readily wrote a letter to the Police. We knew, of course, that the Police would take their own time to investigate, if they did at all, but we had bought some peace, for the time being at any rate.

All the trouble I had to face on the estate had an interesting upshot though. Horrocks was a law-abiding man and he would not lightly disregard a Company rule. But, he felt bound to help me. One day, I received a letter from him that he had personally typed out himself on his own typewriter. He said that due to the steepness of the land on Ranikoil, and for facilitating better supervision, I was to use my motorcycle on the division while going about my work, at all times henceforth including the morning hours, and that he was advising the General Manager accordingly. Horrocks had felt that I had to have dignity in the eyes of the labour, and he was going to give me all the help he could. And, for a start, I would ride around, not walk like all the others did. Since that day, all the Assistant Superintendents who subsequently joined the Company could use their motorcycles – supplied by the Company – throughout the day.

By the time I joined, Horrocks had served the Company for thirty years. The Coonoor Club in The Nilgiris landed both Horrocks and me our jobs in SITE. A few months before Horrocks signed up with the Company, his father, Dr O Horrocks, had met JA Richardson – that man JAR again – in the Coonoor Club and asked him if his son, Oswald William, could become a planter. JAR told him that his brother-in-law, Wilkie, probably had a vacancy for an Assistant in his Company, SITE, and asked the young Horrocks to send him an application. There was indeed a billet available as JAR had thought, and Horrocks got the job.

Both Horrocks and I drank gin, in some quantity. I drank Hayward's Piccadilly Gin which at thirteen rupees a bottle was something that I could afford on my pay, while Horrocks imbibed Carew's, priced at eighteen rupees a bottle. Every rupee mattered. After we came to know each other rather well, we'd meet at each other's bungalow every now and again. And, we hardly ever talked shop. Quite surprisingly, more often than not, we talked about the English language. Horrocks was very particular about the way in which English should be spoken. He was fond of saying that the only two things that mattered were good health and a good accent. And he spoke English with an impeccable accent. He told me once that he wasn't highly educated, but that he had decided that he would learn to speak English with a good accent. And he did. In the olden days, a good way to acquire a good English accent was to listen to the BBC English news broadcast. A couple of newsreaders whose names I can remember even today were George Eason and Pamela Crichton. There were some others who were equally good, but their names elude me. Practically all the British planters and their wives listened to the BBC news at 9.30 pm before turning in for the night. Horrocks remarked once that regional accents were starting to creep in. He certainly would not have approved of some of the accents that are a regular feature of BBC broadcasts today. Ever generous, Horrocks even went on to tell people that *I* was teaching *him* English, all because I happened to know what a pyrrhic victory meant!

I hardly ever went out anywhere after work. There was usually a blazing log fire in the hearth in the sitting room, and I would sit in front of it and have my tea. When I finished my tea, and if I didn't have any social engagements, my cook-butler would remove my tea tray and place my bottle of gin and a jug of water within easy reach. He would then go away until it was time for me to have my bath and dinner. Fortunately, this particular chap didn't drink unlike the previous one I'd hired, but he helped himself to some of my other provisions. There is absolutely nothing more heart-warming than sitting in front of a good fire, sipping gin and reading. Needless to say, I never lacked for reading material. But there is only so much reading one can do, and boredom soon reared its ugly head again.

Drinking gin became a necessity. As the last line of a popular ditty went, it was one way of drowning my sorrows. Nothing is more heartbreaking than a dreary, dull, daily routine. The recalcitrant labour didn't help matters either. Like the two geese on Glenmary division, I wanted out. And the sooner, the better.

One evening, when my morale was at a particularly low ebb, I saw through my alcoholic haze an advertisement in the daily newspaper offering Short Service Commissions to retired Army officers if they were otherwise eligible. I applied at once. In due course, I was asked to appear before a panel of officers specially constituted for the purpose at the Army Headquarters in New Delhi.

The call came at the end of the Company's financial year when I had practically no leave to my credit. I had exhausted most of my leave by going to Madras at the height of the monsoon to escape the heavy rains in Peermade. I also had very little money, and could think of going to Delhi only by train. There was only one train to Delhi from Madras called the Grand Trunk Express, and it took all of forty eight hours. But I had to get to Madras first, which meant going by bus to Madura, then taking the train to Madras. Further, I had to spend a whole day in Madras before boarding the train to Delhi. When I came to Cochin for my interview with Madden, I had flown down from Delhi to Madras as I had enough money for a plane ticket. Living in a field area in the Army, there was very little scope to spend money, so I had a healthy bank balance.

I went to see Horrocks about this latest development. To my great surprise, he didn't turn down my request for leave. Although I was not entitled to any leave, he asked me how many days I wanted. I did a quick calculation and asked for ten days which was cutting it very fine. Horrocks never broke any rule if he could help it, yet, to my astonishment, he wrote to the General Manager informing him that he was sanctioning me ten days' special leave to attend to an important personal matter, which was perfectly true, of course.

I reached Delhi just in time for the interview. The selection panel consisted of three officers, a Sikh Brigadier who was the presiding officer, and two other officers of lower rank. The Brigadier said to me that from the papers in front of him he could see that I was a tea planter in Kerala, and asked if I worked for a British Company. I confirmed it. He then went on to say, "I have stayed in the bungalows of some planters in Munnar in Kerala, and they lead very comfortable lives. I am surprised that you want to come back into the Army." We chatted for a few more minutes. The other two officers said nothing, nor did the Brigadier invite them to ask me any questions. To indicate that the interview was over, the presiding officer told me to get myself medically examined by a panel of Army doctors before getting back.

I had very little doubt that I would be selected. I had to spend a whole day in Madras before catching a train for Madura in the evening, so I went to see my father who lived in Padappai, a village about an hour or so away. He did not disapprove of my intention to return to the Army but only asked if Madden would let me go. He was prescient.

Some time after I got back to Peermade, I heard from the Army Headquarters. I had been granted a Short Service Commission, and had to join a unit posted in Orissa forthwith. I went to see Horrocks in the evening and showed him the letter. Practically all the able-bodied British planters in the district had volunteered to serve their king and country during the Second World War, and Horrocks was no exception. He reminisced about his own time in the Army, and also said that it was not at all odd that I should want to give up planting. He told me that he kept a black book in which he wrote down the names of all the men who came to plant in the Peermade-Vandiperiyar district. The turnover was so rapid – forty five men had left in less than seven years – that he gave up keeping a record.

Horrocks himself had felt at one time that he was not cut out to be a planter. He was an ace motor mechanic, so when he went to England on his first home leave after five and a half years in Peermade, he joined a motor garage to see if he would fit in there. He got paid very little money, barely enough to buy himself a few buns and a couple of cups of tea each day. So he decided to come back to Peermade in spite of the many drawbacks of being a planter here. He stayed for thirty nine years and a bit. Some stamina.

We talked for a long time and, inevitably, imbibed a lot too. Horrocks then said that if I was leaving Peermade because I was unhappy, he could safely bet that I would be unhappy wherever I went. That evening, I left without taking a firm decision.

A few days later, Madden, as the General Manager, came on an official visit to Ladrum. He first went round my division. Horrocks and I accompanied him. It was all over in a couple of hours, and rather unexpectedly, Madden said to Horrocks, "Let's go up to Davidar's bungalow for a smoke before we go any farther." So, the three of us rode up to my bungalow.

Madden saw a tin of Gold Flake cigarettes on my mantelpiece. They were expensive cigarettes, and I remember my father used to smoke them before he retired from the judiciary. I really can't recall why I kept those cigarettes there that day, but I'm sure I was not trying to show off because I hadn't the foggiest that Madden would come up to my bungalow – it was not on the programme. Moreover, by this time I had switched from Capstan Navy Cut priced at three rupees for a tin of fifty cigarettes to the much cheaper Berkeley, which at one rupee fourteen annas a tin was more affordable – we hadn't gone metric yet. Madden said he hadn't smoked a Gold Flake in a long time, and declared, "I am going to smoke one of your Gold Flakes, Davidar."

Barely had Madden lit up and sat down, when Horrocks said to him, "Davidar has been offered a Short Service Commission in the Army, and he is thinking of accepting it." Madden turned to me and said, "And, where have you been

posted?" I told him some place in Orissa. He said, "I'll tell you
what, I'll give you some special leave. You go and quietly have
a look around the place. If you don't like it, you may not go." I
was made to feel wanted.

And then, quite suddenly, Madden remembered that the
Ranikoil bungalow could do with some improvement. It
certainly could. At least three Englishmen, including a retired
Major from the British Army, had lived in that bungalow before
I did. They were all married, yet none of them had asked for it
to be made a little more comfortable.

The bungalow had just one bedroom, and a tin tub in the
bathroom. When I was posted to Ranikoil, Mrs Madden
warned me about the lintel of the bathroom door, which was
so low I could bang my head against it. I couldn't think how
anyone conceived of such an idea.

Anyway, in the short discussion that followed, it was
decided that the bungalow would be renovated and improved.
An extra bedroom would be added, and it would adjoin the
existing one. The bathroom would be common to both, and it
would be modernized, complete with a new door to replace
the old one. Madden also instructed Horrocks to provide
adequate furniture for the new bedroom, and asked him to
send an estimate for everything as soon as possible. All the
improvements were soon sanctioned, and the Board accepted
Madden's recommendations *in toto*. It was all very comfortable
when the work was finished. Madden seemed anxious to retain
me, and my successors to the bungalow benefited.

It was time to review my options, and it took me a couple
of days. Even as I wrestled with the feeling that I would be a
cad if I left after all that was being done to make me physically
comfortable, it was a case of physical comfort against remaining
mentally unhappy. Mental happiness won, and I decided to
leave. On the day I made up my mind, I went to see Horrocks
in the evening. We sat and chatted for a long time, drinking
our favourite tipple. Before I could tell him why I had come to

see him, Horrocks must have sensed my mission and said that he would be personally sorry if I left. I don't know if it was all the gin I had imbibed, but I felt I would be letting him down if I left after what he said. That is how I decided to stay.

It was probably soon after this that a pleasant interlude came my way. Harry Hewitt, the Superintendent of an estate called Stagbrook, died rather unexpectedly of a perforated duodenal ulcer. Stagbrook belonged to another sterling Company, but was administered by the General Manager of my Company. Although I had only about two years' service, Madden placed me in acting charge of Stagbrook until the Board of Directors of that Company in London decided on the next move. He also gave me a small acting allowance which was most welcome.

Hewitt was an extremely nice man. He had been a planter in Malaya (as Malaysia was then known) before he came to Peermade. He was a bachelor and looked rather old. Although small-made, he had been a champion tennis player in Malaya, and played the most delectable tennis. He wasn't too quick on the tennis court, but when he got to the ball, he could do just about what he pleased with it. In the dry weather, I played a lot of tennis in the Peermade Club. As I was relatively young, I played a rather energetic game as someone remarked.

I was attracted to tennis while I was still in school. An uncle, George Mathuram, played an extremely good and stylish game. His father, A Mathuram, my maternal grandfather, was a very wealthy man. He was a qualified allopathic doctor, but made his fortune, and continued to make it, by patenting the ayurvedic medicines that he had formulated. My grandfather's *Guru* medicines were highly efficacious, and apart from South India, they were most popular in Ceylon and in some of the other eastern countries like Malaya where a number of Tamils lived, mostly labourers on the tea and rubber plantations. My grandfather lived in a palatial house set in about ten acres of prime land in Trichinopoly, and there was a tennis court on the property, an unheard-of luxury in those distant days. My uncle, who studied law in Madras and later apprenticed at a firm of solicitors there, came to Trichinopoly for a couple of months every summer and played tennis every evening with a paid Marker. I would sit and watch him playing, totally entranced. He had a kicking topspin second serve which was the first time I had seen one.

Seeing that I was interested in tennis, my uncle encouraged me. In fact, he got me my first tennis racket. I did not receive any special coaching, but the Marker would teach me the rudiments of the game when he was free. Neither did I have too many opportunities to play the game until I joined the Army where I played a lot of tennis during my first year. I could hit the ball somewhat, but my service was always my weak point.

Hewitt saw me play tennis in the Peermade Club and said that I had the potential to play a decent game, except that my service was poor. He took me out on the court on a few occasions and tried to teach me to serve. In spite of his rather short stature, Hewitt had the same kicking topspin serve that my uncle had, which was almost unplayable. Unfortunately, Hewitt passed away before he could teach me to serve properly. Rod Laver, the only man to win all the four Grand Slam titles in one year twice, arguably the greatest tennis player ever, always reminded me of Hewitt, probably because they were built alike.

Stagbrook bungalow was rather large but very poorly lit. Its supply of electricity came from the generator in the factory which was some distance away. As a result, the lighting in most of the rooms, including the sitting room, was very dim. Reading at night was out of the question. When I went to bed at night, I had to switch off the sitting room light and walk along a long, narrow passage in the dark before getting to my bedroom.

Having heard of haunted houses, I was naturally apprehensive about occupying Stagbrook bungalow so soon after Hewitt had died. I worried a little about whether his ghost would accost me while I was making my way to the bedroom in the dark.

The idea of someone's ghost haunting the house in which he had lived is not totally far-fetched. There is the recorded instance of a British planter called Pascoe, a bachelor, who was known to haunt his old house somewhere in The Nilgiris. When someone moved into his bungalow, he would pay the new occupant a visit at night, but for some reason, only on the first night. And, his was a benign ghost that meant no harm to anyone.

There is this other story, a true one, which George Joseph, a close friend, told me. George was the Superintendent of Pambanar Estate which belonged to TTE, the other British Company with estates in the district. Brigton Estate, which later became a part of Pambanar Estate and TTE, was originally owned and developed by a retired Dutch sea captain. The Manager's bungalow on Pambanar was built by this Dutchman, who had apparently incorporated parts of his brig into the bungalow.

George, then a bachelor, was to attend a party one night in a friend's bungalow many miles away. A couple he was friendly with were to accompany him, but they lived some distance away in Vandiperiyar. While he waited for his friends, George got a fire going in his sitting room. When they arrived, George asked his bungalow servants to put out the fire, and the good lady also remarked that they didn't want another Glenmary bungalow episode (referring to the bungalow in which I had lived that had burnt down not so long ago). To make doubly certain that nothing would ignite and cause a fire when they were away, George poured a whole jugful of water over the embers. They left after making sure that the fire was put out completely, and no logs were left in the hearth.

When they returned several hours later, George thought he saw a light in the sitting room of his bungalow as he turned off the main road. He raced home. On reaching the bungalow, he flung open his sitting room door and saw, to his utter amazement, a beautiful fire blazing away in the hearth. The bungalow servants couldn't throw any light on the matter when George questioned them about it the next morning.

Legend has it that every night, a servant used to light a fire for the Dutch sea captain in his sitting room. This servant had, apparently, died in service, and his ghost was heard lighting the fire on several nights. No occupant of Pambanar bungalow had ever seen the ghosts of the Dutch sea captain or his faithful servant, nor did the two ever bother anyone in any way. But the fire burning in the hearth served to keep their memory alive.

As a little boy, I used to be very afraid of the dark and of ghosts. The fear was not inborn but was instilled in me. In the early years of his judicial service, my father was posted to a town called Kumbakonam where my parents rented a large house. For two years, my older brother and I studied there in a well-known high school, which was rather close to where we lived, before going back to Trichinopoly to continue with our studies. My father was a champion bridge player, and he would set out every evening in his car (a Baby Ford, as it was called) to play bridge at the Club which was quite some distance from our house. By the time my father returned, more often than not, my brothers and I had finished our dinner and were ready for bed. We slept in a large bedroom upstairs, and as we were quite small, my mother would send a peon who was on night duty to sit with us until we fell asleep. One of my father's peons specialized in telling us salacious stories. I hardly understood what they meant because I was barely ten years of age. Another man told us some frightening ghost stories – about how ghosts attacked you in the dark – stories that had a huge impact on me. I prayed earnestly to God to save me from those horrible creatures, and crossed myself all over before dropping off. Childhood impressions last a long time.

Eventually, as I grew up, and especially after I joined the Army, I got over my fear. However, I was a little fearful all the same of encountering Hewitt in the Stagbrook bungalow. But I needn't have worried. Hewitt must have liked me, so he left me alone.

I liked working on Stagbrook. It was a sprawling estate even though the tea itself was nothing to rave about. I had nobody to report to, and there was no labour trouble. Since I wanted to get to every part of the estate on my motorcyle, I converted practically all the footpaths on the estate into motorcycle tracks. After a month on the estate, Madden came to visit, to see how I was getting on. Leading the way on my bike, I took Madden all over the estate. He was very pleased that he could go anywhere in Stagbrook on his motorcycle.

Unfortunately for me, a retired planter, WAJ Milner, was sent out from England to take charge of the estate. It was a compassionate posting. He had been a man of some consequence in his working days, and was extremely well thought of. He had held the post of the Honorary Secretary and the Chairman of the District Planters' Association for several years in each position. He had even been the Chairman of UPASI for a year.

About a year earlier, he had retired from TTE. He didn't seem a fit man even then, and was obviously a shadow of his former self now. At his farewell, I was sitting next to him in the front hall of the Peermade Club where ballroom dancing was going on. Everybody on the dance floor was European. Hewitt was also there. Milner said to me, "You see all those chaps jumping about. Not one of them has a house in England but I have." It was said that Milner's second wife, who had a grown-up son of her own, had cruelly taken his house away from him. As his future looked bleak, Milner had gone to the Secretaries of Stagbrook Estate, and they had sent him out to Peermade to take charge of it. By this time, Milner had become old and decrepit. He didn't have any transport, so he hardly went round the estate. Nobody seemed to mind, as the estate was going to be sold anyhow. A few years later, Milner died in Peermade of cerebral thrombosis, and was buried in the grounds of St George's Church which was next door to Stagbrook Estate.

After handing over charge to Milner, I went back to Ranikoil. I was originally slated to return to Glenmary Estate after one year on Ranikoil, but the situation on the labour front had not quite returned to normal. So Madden decided, quite rightly, that I should spend another year on Ranikoil, and gain reasonable control of the labour, lest they thought they had driven me away. By then, an uneasy truce had been declared by all concerned on the division, and the rest of my stay on Ranikoil was quite uneventful.

∾

Birds in Trees and Fireflies at Night

After my two-year stint on Ranikoil mercifully came to an end, I was posted back to Glenmary Estate, but this time around, I was in charge of Woodlands, an outlying division. The bungalow on this division commanded a magnificent view and was tucked well away from the labour lines, unlike in Ranikoil where I lived within earshot of the living quarters of the workers who quarrelled loudly practically every night. There was a red gum and scrub jungle just behind it. The day after I moved into the Woodlands bungalow, I awoke in the morning to the belling of a sambar in the jungle, very close by. Everything seemed so peaceful.

The routine on this division was the same as anywhere else. It was not long before I didn't know how to keep myself sufficiently occupied during my hours of duty. One day, I went to the Head Office to meet Madden, whom I knew I could approach at any time. I told him that I was nearly at the end of my tether, and was again seriously thinking of quitting. He tried to jolly me along, and said that my prospects in the Company were excellent, and in due course, I would end up in McIntyre's position, the No.2 man. At that time, an Indian in the top job of a British Company was quite unthinkable. As by this time Madden and I were good friends, I could tell him frankly that what I could become in the distant future didn't interest me so much as what I was to do with myself in the harrowing present. He became sentimental and told me with a faraway look in his eyes how he enjoyed working on my division (where he had stayed for a long time) when he was in sole independent charge of it a couple of decades ago, and how the bungalow in which I lived owed much to him. Since the Company was apparently committed to having at least one Indian on its Executive Staff, Madden tried to encourage me to stay.

He also said, seriously, "There is money in this racket (his words)." This remark was a bit tongue-in-cheek as he was probably thinking of himself and not me. I felt that he could have looked after me better, as I had reason to believe that Madden controlled my pay, not the Board, as they were yet to get used to the idea of having an Indian Executive on their payroll.

Only the previous year, rewards were distributed for the huge profit the Company had made the preceding year. Shareholders were allotted a generous 1:1 bonus issue, and the Executives on the ground received an ad hoc increase in pay. I don't know how much Madden himself was given, but the two senior Superintendents (of whom Horrocks was one) were each given a hefty raise of five hundred rupees more per month, the junior Superintendent (Richardson) two hundred and fifty, the other assistant, an expatriate, one hundred, and I was given fifty rupees. The manner in which the remuneration was graded indicated that the Board must have received some help from the General Manager on the spot, although, in all fairness, it cannot be conclusively proved. Horrocks, my Superintendent on Ladrum, told me that I deserved to be awarded more than I was actually given. He had first-hand knowledge of the work that I did, and in terms of pure physical energy expended, I left the others standing as I was doing what the English farmers did in their fields.

Madden told me that he could spend a lot of time in the nursery, watching the plants grow and carrying out all kinds of experiments like how long it took a bud to grow into a leaf. I promised I'd seriously try and emulate his ways. Every morning, religiously, I would go to the nursery and commune with my plants for a long time as I had official permission to do so. They didn't inspire me. I would then stroll to a deep pool in a stream nearby and watch the fish in its pellucid waters. The fish had vertical black and white stripes, like a zebra's, and I hadn't seen fish like them anywhere before. However, you could only stand and watch the fish for so long. It was no good.

I went back to the General Manager with my woes. By tradition, the General Manager of the Company was also the Superintendent of the Company's Group Hospital, Woodlands Hospital, which was situated on my division. Madden told me that he would make me the Superintendent of the hospital, and he would notify the estates accordingly. The Medical Officer of the hospital was Dr Ganapathy, a retired Surgeon Lieutenant Commander of the Indian Navy. He was a delightful man. He graciously accepted my appointment as the hospital Superintendent, and we got on extremely well. The hospital was close to the muster ground on my division, so every evening after muster, I would go along to the hospital to see Dr Ganapathy. Probably by force of habit, Madden would drive up in his car practically every evening, and the three of us would have an amicable chat before he drove away.

Madden also decided, on an impulse, that I should take over the payments in the Glenmary Estate office from Richardson, the Superintendent, so that I would have some more work to do. Richardson, who guarded his responsibilities jealously, would have none of it. He said he couldn't run the office with me disrupting his work by opening and shutting his safe to make payments. I could see his point of view, and agreed with him entirely. It was very much part of the Superintendent's duties to handle the estate safe, and I was glad that Richardson didn't want to part with it. It was Madden's idea, and the arrangement could have caused much friction and unhappiness.

I decided to make the best of a bad job, and continued to live one day at a time. Rather unhappily, Richardson and I fell out a few months later over a trivial matter. Before it could assume an alarming proportion, Madden transferred me to Kuduakarnam Estate, the third estate in the company, as its Assistant Superintendent.

Luckily for me, another young Englishman was sent out from England as an Assistant Superintendent. His name was Richard de Lancy Walters, but he came to be known simply as Dick Walters. Dick was very young, extremely well-mannered, soft-spoken and of excellent pedigree, and had been educated in a good Public School in England.

There was really no vacancy when Dick arrived. He was due to take my place on Woodlands when I moved to Kuduakarnam. As there was no bungalow to accommodate him, he stayed for a month with Richardson on Glenmary Estate. By this time, I was reckoned a senior Assistant Superintendent as I had been with the Company for three years. Richardson had neither the time nor the inclination to train Dick Walters, so he passed him on to me, saying that I should 'teach' him whatever I knew about tea planting as required by the Company.

Dick came over to Woodlands every morning after breakfast on his motorcycle, and spent the whole day with me. In the evening after tea, he would go back to the Superintendent's bungalow for dinner, bed and breakfast. Dick was athletic and was as interested in sports and games as I was. We spent much time talking about them, and when I remembered, I gave him 'lessons' in tea planting as I was told to do.

Like most of us did, Dick started eating his heart out quite early on. But he decided to do something about it, instead of sitting around moping. On some days, though, when the sun came out in all its glory after a heavy spell of rain, and everything glistened and the birds twittered in the trees, Dick would think that a tea estate in Peermade was not such a bad place after all. But he would quickly admonish himself to not weaken. Actually, there were times when a tea estate could cast a spell over you. My daughter remembers to this day the fireflies in the trees at night which looked like tiny bulbs on a Christmas tree. For me, the spectacle on Glenmary Estate of small minivets, the male birds in black, grey and orange-crimson, and the females with yellow in the place of orange-crimson, flitting about on a sunny morning in the *Albizzia* trees that we grew for shade in the tea, is a sight I still cherish very much. You could not hope to see a prettier display of colour and light anywhere.

Dick had a head for figures and felt that he would do better as an accountant than as a tea planter. He subscribed to a correspondence course in accountancy in England, and did his lessons diligently. Even after Dick left Woodlands and went to Ranikoil, we continued to see each other. We also played a lot of tennis together in the Club. As we were the only two Assistants in the Company, Madden and his wife would invite us to some of their parties. At one such party, we were both standing in a corner of the sitting room sipping our drinks, when Dick said to me, "I hate to drink the man's whisky when I have to tell him sooner or later that I am packing it in." Dick had already booked his passage to Australia from where he planned to return to England after a few months. But he didn't know how to break the news to Madden.

The opportunity Dick had been waiting for came about rather unexpectedly. Madden liked to plan his life meticulously down to the last detail, well in advance, and unlike for most of us, it seemed to work for him. When Dick still had about a year before he went on his furlough, Madden asked him if he had made any arrangements yet. Dick screwed up the courage to say, "Oh, yes, I am leaving in three months' time actually. For good." That was probably one of the few times that Madden had nothing to say except, "Oh!"

∽

Malabar Police and Spies

The Superintendent of Kuduakarnam Estate was a man called Donald McIntyre. He was another old-timer and the No.2 of the Company, designated the senior Superintendent. He kept himself to himself.

McIntyre was taciturn by nature. I went to see him in his office only when it was absolutely necessary to consult him about something that had to be done on my division. Otherwise, we pretty much kept out of each other's way. He didn't seem to know anything about me, even though I had been with the Company for three years and a bit. Further, knowing Madden, I am pretty certain that when I was first appointed he would have sent out a circular – he was sending out circulars for everything – concerning me, but given McIntyre's attitude, I am almost sure that he would not have read it too closely. About once in three months, an English padre, who was also the English Professor in a Christian college in Kottayam (a town in the plains which served as our base, fifty miles from Peermade), would come up on a Sunday to conduct a service in English at the St George's Church. One Sunday, sometime after I moved to Kuduakarnam, I went to church on my motorcycle, and most of the British planters were there. The next day, I met McIntyre in the field. He said that he saw me in church the previous day, and had he known that I was a Christian, he would have given me a lift in his car!

In McIntyre's room in the office, just above his head, Winston Churchill glowered down from a familiar portrait on the wall. (Churchill was, incidentally, against the dismantling of the British Empire but was respected for his candour and speaking his mind). Occasionally, when I had to meet McIntyre to receive some special instruction, I would go to his office straight after morning muster, and wait outside until the daily morning ritual that took place there was over. It was a stage production in itself. The Head Clerk sat by a window which gave him a clear view of the road that led down from the Superintendent's bungalow to the office, and he would keep looking anxiously for the boss man to appear. When he did, almost exactly at the same time every day, the Head Clerk would give the other clerks in the office a signal. They would then gather in a semicircle at the open door which separated the Superintendent's room from the main office. As McIntyre entered his room, they would all bow and salaam him and say in unison, "Good Morning, Sir." McIntyre would acknowledge their obeisance with a nod of his head and a muted greeting. The clerks would then return to their seats, and he wouldn't see any of them again until the next morning, unless he had to. McIntyre only dealt with the Head Clerk on matters pertaining to the office. It was almost like in the days of the Raj.

In the morning, after attending to matters in the office, McIntyre would walk round the estate. He preferred to walk even though the Company had supplied him with a motorcycle like everybody else, a green Francis-Barnett. He rarely talked to anybody as he walked about. When McIntyre wanted to visit my division, he would walk sedately – for all to see – down the lorry road which led through the fields to the bottom of the division which shared a boundary with Ladrum Estate. His car would be waiting there around midday to take him back to the bungalow for lunch, stopping briefly at the factory which was on the way. The routine never varied.

Like most of the other senior planters in the district, McIntyre was also sarcastic about Madden's ways. When it came to talking about Madden, McIntyre would open up a little, even to me, an Indian. Madden probably knew what the others thought of him, but he couldn't care less. He once told me that his brass neck took him everywhere. It was certainly true.

It was widely known that Madden had spies everywhere to report on his Executive Staff. McIntyre had an interesting take on this. He told me once that if Madden found out something about me, what could he really do? His line of argument was that if Madden confronted me with what he'd heard, and I asked him who the informer was, he couldn't really divulge the identity of the spy, could he?

McIntyre went on to tell me – a rare indulgence – that when he first started planting on some estate near Coonoor in The Nilgiris, he and a friend regularly beat it up somewhere or the other (it was difficult to believe that he could, knowing the man as I did, but then he was also young once). Reports of their escapades reached England, and he and his friend were taken to task. They put their heads together to think who could possibly be passing on the information. They arrived at the conclusion that it had to be the local sub-postmaster who knew the Company's address in England, and who was apparently keeping tabs on them. They duly met with the man, and expressed themselves freely about his character and his ancestry. Not entirely to their surprise, the periodical upbraiding that they received from their bosses stopped completely.

On certain days in the afternoon, the estate *kaddai* man (shopkeeper) on Kuduakarnam would set out in the direction of the Head Office dressed in spotless white clothes. If I met him on the way, he would wish me and give me a sickly smile. One day after lunch, I was riding my motorcycle to work, when I saw the *kaddai* man standing outside his shop, looking up at the top road on which I was. As soon as he spotted me, I saw him glancing at his watch. I knew at once that he had been put on my tail, and had been asked to report on my work habits. The man worshipped Madden, and even many years after Madden left Peermade, he always spoke in glowing terms about his old boss. I wonder what the man's reward was.

Madden had a pet Conductor on Ladrum Estate where Horrocks was the Superintendent. The Conductor was instructed to keep an eye on Horrocks and report on him. When he came to know about it, Horrocks promptly transferred the man to a division from where he couldn't watch him. Horrocks was a man of honour. Once when I was his Assistant on Ranikoil, I saw him going down to the bottom of the division on his motorcycle. I was in a field far above the road, and thinking he might want to see me about something, I came down. He did indeed wish to meet me. He said he could easily have gone to my bungalow and asked the servants there if they knew where I might be, but felt I would think that he was spying on me if I found out that he had done so. He wanted to avoid giving me that impression, so he came looking for me in the field instead.

I didn't have to worry about anyone spying on me as I had an uncompromising conscience. In the daily newspaper that I used to read, there was a cartoon serial about a Chinese sage called Ching Chow. One day the cartoon depicted Ching Chow resting comfortably and saying, 'A clear conscience makes a soft pillow'. Mine was a soft pillow. I kept regular hours and believed in leading by example. Even after I became the No.1 of the Company, I never went home before the factory siren sounded in the evening to indicate the end of a day's work.

Spying was apparently not confined to my Company alone. A European Assistant in TTE, the other British Company in the area, told me once that when his No.1 was on a visit to the estate, he saw him talking quietly to one of the supervisors, out of earshot. He instinctively knew that the man was passing on information about him. When the big man left, he said that he made it quite clear to the Supervisor that he would fix him if he reported on him again.

Rudyard Kipling received the Nobel Prize for literature in 1907, the first Englishman to do so. The Great Game that he wrote about in his masterpiece, the novel *Kim*, was alive

and well in a small way in Peermade-Vandiperiyar fifty
years later.

Life on Kuduakarnam was pretty humdrum. Even the
labour was relatively docile. In the afternoons, after they had
completed their allotted tasks, the men would go away. In the
dry weather, even the women would knock off early as they
had very little leaf to pluck. As a result, with nobody around
in the fields, there was usually nothing to do. At such times, I
would take a book with me and go to a remote corner of the
division where I would sit on my motorcycle and read until it
was time to attend evening muster.

One afternoon, my bike was resting on a bank and I was
sitting on it, reading. A couple of workers appeared suddenly
from nowhere, and walked past me in silence. As they cleared
the bend in the road, but still within my hearing, I heard one
chap tell the other, "Did you see that fellow? We waste our
spare time and he spends his reading. That's the difference
between him and us."

But dull as life was, one incident stands out in my memory
for the sheer drama of it. There was an industry-wide strike
on some big issue. I think it was probably over the payment of
annual bonus which was a contentious issue much of the time.
We had been plucking until the day before the strike. Quite a
lot of green leaf was lying unprocessed on the withering racks
in the factory. A couple of days later, some of the loyal workers
– and there were always some – came and volunteered to
manufacture the leaf for us as it was still just about possible to
do so. We agreed, even though there was an element of risk
attached to it.

The General Manager was on furlough, and McIntyre was
acting for him as was the custom then, while continuing his
normal work as the Superintendent. That day, as the Head of
the Company, McIntyre had to attend a meeting of the senior
planters in the district to discuss the strike situation. I was left
behind to hold the fort. Everything seemed normal for a while.

And then, I saw some fellows assembling outside the factory. It didn't take me too long to establish that they were the union leaders on the estate with their supporters. They started shouting slogans and uttering dire threats to the men inside the factory. Gradually, a crowd began to gather, and they far outnumbered the poor volunteers inside, who were – and, who could blame them? – becoming more and more agitated by the minute.

In less than an hour, the factory siren would signal the start of the lunch break. The crowd outside the factory was distinctively menacing, and the situation was becoming uglier. I was at a loss as to what to do. But I knew that a contingent of the famed Malabar Special Police was stationed in readiness at the Peermade Police Station to deal with any emergency relating to law and order that might arise during the strike. They also went out on patrol every day in a large police van. Fortunately, I had a telephone in my bungalow, so I sped all the way there, and rang the Police Station. I identified myself, and told them about the potentially explosive situation on Kuduakarnam. I then asked if the police patrol could be dispatched to my estate as we needed their help badly. I was informed that they were out, and the staff in the Police Station said that they had no means of communicating with the police patrol, but thought that they might be coming towards my estate. A police van had never before come to Kuduakarnam Estate, located as it was at a dead end. What hope had I then that the police patrol would show up now? I went back and kept watch from a spot that provided a good view of what was going on outside the factory. The crowd was milling about and noisy. The siren was due to sound at any time now. I was desperate.

I don't think I prayed, but God must have seen my plight and decided to send succour. I thought I heard a heavy vehicle in the distance. And it wasn't my imagination at work. A heavy vehicle was actually coming towards my estate, and the sound of it was growing louder by the minute. I rode out in the direction of the rumbling noise, and just couldn't believe my eyes. It was the blue police van with the men of the Malabar Special Police inside. I met it almost at the place where the road started to descend towards the factory. There was just this one police van to patrol the whole of the rather extensive Peermade-Vandiperiyar district. It could have gone anywhere that day, but for it to come right into Kuduakarnam Estate which was tucked away and not easily accessible, could not have been anything but Divine intervention.

I stopped the van and quickly explained the situation to the Havildar of the contingent. He just said, "Lead the way." I took them down to the factory. The union leaders looked dismayed when they saw the police van coming to a halt outside the factory. The Havildar asked me who the ringleader was. I pointed him out. The Havildar went up to him and said quietly, "I hear you and your friends are going to beat up the men inside the factory when they come out. Is it true?" There was complete silence. The Havildar wasn't finished. He taunted the man some more.

Meanwhile, the two doors at the back of the police van were flung open. There were two rows of men inside, sitting ramrod-straight on benches, facing each other and staring unblinkingly ahead. They wore steel helmets and held heavy lathis in their right hands. The Malabar Special Police were impressive-looking men. The Havildar asked me to arrange for the siren to be sounded. At the same time, he barked out an order. The policemen leapt out of the van and took up positions in various parts of the crowd with their lathis by their sides, at the ready, while still looking straight ahead.

The men inside the factory came out, looking very relieved. The Havildar told them to go home and not be afraid. As they left, he turned to the ringleader and his mates and said, "Now go away and be good chaps. If I hear that you have been naughty again, I'll come back and knock the living daylights out of you. Have I made myself clear?" He watched them slink away. I thanked him profusely for his timely help but he just said that he was only doing his duty. The Malabar Special Police were reputed for their cold efficiency and ruthlessness, and I was privileged to see them in action, even if only on a limited scale. Just that precise moment, the Superintendent returned. McIntyre couldn't have timed his return better.

About this time, an unexpected development arose. I received a letter from a very senior British planter, who had been in independent charge of an estate – which was also the only one his Company owned in that area – for more than a quarter century. He simply said that if I came the following Saturday to the Club in the evening, I would hear something to my advantage. Cryptic but intriguing.

This gentleman had grown bulky with age but was still fond of his tennis. He must have liked the way I played my tennis, vigorously if nothing else. When he was the President of the Peermade Club, even though I had been a member for only about two years, he elevated me to the position of number one singles player of our Club in local tournaments, when we met other clubs especially the Vandiperiyar Club. This was before a couple of chaps, George Joseph (the friend who told me about the ghost in his bungalow) and Yash Pal Sarwal came to live and work among us. It was apparent that they had both played a lot of tennis in their young lives because they lifted the game to quite a different level. Much of the time, they battled each other, and some of us older players were relegated to being mere spectators. Playing tennis was never a duel before their arrival on the scene. Many of the senior planters were in their teens and just out of school when they came out to India, so they probably learnt to play tennis in planters' clubs. As a result, points were won more often by chance than by design. But what really mattered was that it was all good fun and everyone had a great time.

Anyway, when I arrived at the Club that Saturday evening at the usual time, this gentleman was already there, waiting for me. As soon as I entered, he ushered me into the 'Gents' and came straight to the point. "Look, I am retiring soon after many years' service. I want to recommend you to take over from me. Will you take the job if it is offered to you?" I was flabbergasted, to put it mildly.

I couldn't tell him that I was actually trying to get out of planting altogether. I had to think, and think quickly too. If I hadn't intended to quit, I would have jumped at the offer as it would not only have been an independent job but a quantum leap for me. But, I had a good excuse to trot out. I had been with my Company for only three years, so I told him that to get even half of the Company's contribution to my Provident Fund (pitiful though it was then), I would have to serve them for at least five years. In the circumstances, much as I appreciated his generous offer, I regretted my inability to accept it. He simply said that he wanted very much for me to succeed him, and was sorry I couldn't.

It so happened that when I turned down the offer to move to another Company, there was an advertisement in the newspaper for sales executives in Bangalore. I decided to apply for the job through an unlikely friend. The Travancore Medical Fund, a medical set-up to which my Company and the other companies with European interests in the district subscribed, had recently appointed a doctor called John Lyn-Jones as their Chief Medical Officer. Lyn-Jones was a quiet and likeable young man, and he was new to India. I do not know how we became good friends but we did. When I was on Ranikoil, every now and then Lyn-Jones would drop in, as he had to pass by my bungalow when visiting some estate or the other in the Vandiperiyar region on official duty.

I didn't want my reply to the advertisement to be routed through the estate office – all letters normally were – in case the clerk in charge got curious and spread the word around. Or, he might even have charged me for postage, pocketed the money and destroyed my letter. There was actually an instance of this particular clerk appropriating the money allocated for postage. Every estate in the Company had to send little, round tin boxes of tea samples to the Company's Tea Brokers in London. The Tea Brokers, in turn, would taste the teas and report on them before putting them up for sale. The Brokers had complained that the samples from Kuduakarnam Estate were not reaching them. When an enquiry was conducted, it was found that the clerk had been charging postage on the samples but was not sending them. He was caught red-handed because with his limited intelligence, he had neatly stacked all the tins that should have gone to London in an open, overhead shelf behind his desk in the office. Rather surprisingly, he was not charged with embezzlement and sacked, but instead was let off with just a warning on account of his father who had retired as a senior staff member after many years of loyal service to the Company.

Anyway, I took my problem to Lyn-Jones and he offered to help. We sat down and drafted my application together. Sometime later, he typed out the letter on his typewriter, and got me to sign it. He then took my application to the Post Office in Peermade and posted it himself. In course of time, I was called for an interview. Once again, leave was a problem. But Bangalore was not too far from Cochin by air, so I took a flight out.

The No.2 of the Company, an Englishman, with the unlikely name of an animal, conducted the interview. I was the only one to be interviewed that day. The man was friendly, and during the course of the interview, he told me that I stood a very good chance of being selected as my name ranked quite at the top of the shortlist. He then rang somebody and had a chat in a low voice. After he hung up, he said that he had been talking to the Chairman of the Company who was indisposed that day. He asked if I could stay over for another day, so that the Chairman could also meet me. I told him that with no leave to my credit, I had to take the early morning flight the next day, so as to get back to the estate by the following evening. He said he understood and asked what my immediate plans were. My Indian Airlines ticket had to be confirmed at their office, so he offered to give me a lift, saying that he had some work in town. We travelled some distance before arriving at the airline office. He chatted all the way there, and shook my hand warmly when he dropped me off. Before he left, he expressed the hope that I would join them soon. I believed him. A few days later, I received a letter from the Company to say that my attempt to secure a job with them was unsuccessful. I could only presume that the Chairman was peeved that I didn't stay on in Bangalore an extra day as he had desired. I was thwarted yet again.

I had a special reason to want to get out at that particular juncture. Madden had gone on furlough to England, and had apparently convinced the Company's Board that I deserved a trip to England. Soon after the Board agreed to his recommendation, Madden wrote to me privately. He explained that the Company would send me to England for two months on an 'official' visit. The trip was termed official for tax purposes, but it also meant that I could be away for only sixty days, from the time I left the country until I returned. To comply with the official requirement of the visit, I was obliged to spend time in the office of the Company's Secretaries every now and then, and periodically attend the office of the Company's Tea Brokers as well. Normally, I would have jumped at this unexpected offer as I had not left the shores of India before. But I was not exactly jubilant. Instead, I was filled with a sense of foreboding. I remembered an Old Testament story that seemed analogous to my situation.

There was this man Jacob, who had indulged in a bit of sharp practice. He had cheated his older brother Esau of his birthright, and was running away from him. His mother, Rebekah, whose pet Jacob was, had advised him to flee to her brother, Laban, and stay there until Esau was ready to forgive him. Laban had two daughters, Leah and Rachael. Rachael, the younger daughter, was much the prettier of the two and Jacob fell in love with her and wanted to marry her. When Laban said to Jacob that he would be paid wages for the work that he did for him, Jacob said that he would work for him for free for seven years if Laban would give him Rachael in marriage. Laban agreed. When Jacob had served Laban for the stipulated period, he asked for Rachael to be given to him as agreed upon. If Jacob was wily, Laban was wilier. When the marriage was arranged, Laban quietly substituted Leah in Jacob's marriage bed. The next morning, when Jacob discovered that Laban had tricked him, he complained. Laban had a ready answer. He said it was not their custom to give the younger daughter in marriage before the older one and asked Jacob to complete one bridal week with Leah, after which he could have Rachael in return for another seven years of service. This time Laban kept his word. After Jacob spent one bridal week with Leah, Laban gave him Rachael also, but Jacob had to work for another seven years for Laban.

As in Jacob's story, I wondered if I would be required to serve the Company for another four years by going to England. I confided my misgivings to Lyn-Jones. He reassured me, saying, that the trip was a reward from the Company in recognition of the hard work that I had put in for four years. He also said that they could not, by right, ask me to serve for another four years by giving me this inducement. I accepted his line of reasoning and felt more at ease.

As the acting General Manager, McIntyre conveyed the Board's decision to me when he came to know of it. He took no further part in it. As far as he was concerned, I could go anywhere.

On his return from furlough, Madden asked me how far I had progressed in preparing for my forthcoming visit to England. I told him that I had applied for my passport and was awaiting further development. He was aghast. He asked me to leave immediately for Madras and not come back without my passport. The idea of a few days free leave appealed to me, so I took off as ordered.

I got to Madras and told my father why I had come down. He offered to accompany me to the Inspector General of Police (IG), the top Police Officer of the State, who was known to the family. My father explained the purpose of our visit to the IG, who, without a moment's hesitation, sent for a Superintendent of Police (SP) working under him, and asked him to arrange for my passport. It was as simple as that. The SP noted down the necessary details, and asked me to go and see him a couple of days later. When I did, he handed me my passport. I didn't get many days of free leave after all.

With so much happening, I also got betrothed, quite unexpectedly, to a very nice girl. My father had to undergo major surgery, so I went to Madras to see him. At that time, my mother and her youngest sister (who had always been fond of me, right from childhood) had arranged for me to meet this girl. Much against my mother's wishes, I kept putting off getting married, as I was not sure how I would support a wife and family without a steady job after I gave up planting as I had hoped to do. Kipling said he travels the fastest who travels alone. I believed it to be true. With marriage in the offing, all thoughts of flight had to be put on hold. It was to be westward-ho in two months' time, willy-nilly.

༄

Passage to London

Lest the reader gets the idea that I was going on a paid holiday to England, I hasten to say it was anything but that. Of course, the Company picked up the tab for a return air ticket, but I had to find the money for all my expenses in England for two months. Madden helped me get over the problem. He gave me a couple of cheques drawn on his bank in London, and also arranged for an account to be opened in my name. In return, he took the equivalent in post-dated rupee cheques from me. It was thirteen rupees to the pound sterling then. It was very good of Madden to part with sterling when nobody who had saved up money in England would do so. But then, it was a matter of honour with him since he had persuaded the Board to get me to England. And he must have known that having done so, he would have to finance me, as without his help, I just could not have made the trip at all. Having handed over the post-dated cheques to Madden to pay for the money he had lent me, I knew that I would have to tighten my belt several holes for some months to come. But that was in the future, and I decided that I would worry about it when the time came. Right now, only the present mattered.

Madden told me that my education in the English way of life must start the moment I took off from India, and that meant flying BOAC (British Overseas Airways Corporation), the forerunner of the present British Airways. The aeroplane that I found myself in was called an Argonaut, a rather small machine compared to the planes which fly long distances these days. My New Oxford Dictionary of English says that the argonaut is a small floating octopus. I don't know how the floating octopus moves, but my flying octopus was quite slow and kept coming down at every opportunity. We took off from Bombay, and came down soon afterwards at Karachi in Pakistan. From then on, it was to be a number of short hops. It huffed and it puffed as it went along, and when it reached Rome airport it gave up the ghost altogether. We were there for many hours, and by the time we reached London, I had a monumental headache.

Quite soon after I reached London in July 1957, the Board sanctioned the Assistants in the Company a bonus of two hundred pounds, as they'd had a good year. I suspect it was meant to induce the other Assistant, a young Englishman who was very unhappy, to stay. But I hope I am terribly wrong. Or perhaps, it was a goodwill gesture on their part to help me during my sojourn in England. Whatever the reason, it was an absolute godsend which even Madden had not anticipated. So, I didn't have to encash Madden's cheques, only the first one, maybe. There was no restriction on making remittances overseas in those days, so Madden arranged for the money to be sent to the bank in London at once.

Through the Board, Madden also arranged my lodging in a very reasonably-priced hotel that a planter friend of his, who had stayed there previously, had told him about. The hotel was in a very nice locality, in South Kensington, and I could afford their tariff. The room was comfortable, and the rate for lodging alone was five pounds a week. The hotel had several storeys but no elevator and, I believe, the further up you went, the cheaper it got. My room was, I think, on the third or fourth floor, but I was fit and didn't mind climbing up to my room at the end of the day. There was a cheap eating place close by, a Lyons Corner shop, where I always had my breakfast before setting forth for the day. And, I was out every day.

My room didn't have an attached bathroom. To get to the water closet (WC), I had to climb down a couple of steps and walk along a covered corridor outside. The bathroom was also nearby. I never found them occupied, so it was all very convenient.

In Peermade, we didn't have any self-locking doors, and if there were any in other parts of the country, I was not aware of them. A few days after I moved in, I walked out of the room one morning and, by force of habit, banged the door shut behind me. I heard an ominous click and discovered that I had locked myself out. I gingerly walked down the stairs to the reception. As it was still very early in the morning, there was fortunately no one about except the man at the reception. I explained my predicament to him, and he came up to my room with the duplicate key and let me in. All went well for a while, and I had to remind myself every time I went to the WC or to the bathroom that my door was self-locking. A few weeks later, I shut the door once again behind me without thinking and had to sneak down for help. Even before I reached the ground floor, the same man looked up from the reception and said, "Oh, no, not again." I said, "I'm afraid so." Thankfully, he was not in a bad mood and forgave me.

Life was good in London. If I was asked which two months in my life I enjoyed the most, I would unhesitatingly say those that I spent in London. My unhappiness as a planter in Peermade disappeared, and I decided to make the most of the present and enjoy myself while I could. London was extremely well signposted, and since I had lived and worked with the British for a few years, I never once felt out of place. I went where I pleased, and didn't experience any rebuffs or rudeness anywhere, although a good friend of mine back in Peermade was worried that I might come across racism in odd places. Obviously, subconsciously, I had picked only the right places to wander in.

While in London, I was obliged to visit the office of the Company's Tea Brokers, Geo.White, Sanderson. I'd go there occasionally and it seemed a friendly place, especially since I had met John Owen, one of the partners, a couple of years earlier when he was in India on his honeymoon. He was a very amiable young man. The staff who sat in an outside room were laid-back, and they always greeted me cheerily and made me welcome.

In that office I met David Kerr (pronounced Carr), a young white man from Kenya. Kerr came, I think, of planting stock, and was in the office of the Tea Brokers to learn tea-tasting. I never once saw David 'spitting' tea but he was generally hanging around. We became good friends. Whenever I appeared, one of the staff members would say, "Ah, Davidar and David Carr are here again," and laugh uproariously at his own rhyming joke. Neither of us was wanted anywhere near the tea-tasting table, so we'd sit around chatting and the odd staff member who happened to be free would join in. A little cockney boy whose job it was to keep everyone in the office supplied with tea to drink, would come along and ask, "Wouldja loik a cuppa tay." Of course, we would, and the little fellow would always provide a refreshing cup of tea.

David must have been in London a while, as he knew a lot about the city. He also had the most desirable knack of making the pound stretch. He would suggest places for us to visit. One day he said, "David, let's go on the Thames." And so, on the Thames we went, in one of those motor launches. Our destination was Greenwich, that time place.

A most fantastic sight awaited us in Greenwich. It was the *Cutty Sark*, the last of the tea clippers and now a tourist attraction. It was kept in excellent condition, spick and span wherever you looked. David and I walked reverently around the clipper before getting back.

Tea was transported from China in clippers, which were sleek and built for speed. Surprisingly, the Americans were the first to introduce the idea of tea clippers. Before the clippers came on the scene, tea was carried by *East Indiamen* which were also called the tea wagons. They were not noted for going at speed, at any speed. The first American clipper to capture the imagination of the British public and the Admiralty alike was *The Oriental* which docked in London in December 1850. The British were not slow to follow suit.

The new season's teas that reached the London market first commanded the best prices, as much as six pence more per pound than the teas that came later – a considerable difference in price. Practically all the ships loaded with tea left the Chinese ports at more or less the same time, so they tended to arrive in London one after another in quick succession. Thus, the tradition was established for the clippers to race each other all the way, and handsome bonuses were paid to the first ship that reached London.

The best known race of all took place in 1866 when sixteen ships left China for Britain at about the same time. The clipper *Ariel* at eight hundred and fifty two tons was the favourite, while *Taeping* at seven hundred and sixty seven tons was not far behind. Both these clippers raced each other all the way, and ninety nine days and eleven thousand miles later, *Taeping* docked just twenty minutes ahead of *Ariel*. *Ariel* had in fact arrived first at the channel, but *Taeping* was lucky to get the steam tug ahead of its rival.

The *Cutty Sark*, which probably would have become the greatest tea clipper ever, came a little late on the scene in the year 1869, the same year that the Suez Canal was opened. Steamers could pass through the Suez Canal and didn't have to wait to catch the wind to make progress, so they cornered all the cargoes, leaving nothing for the clippers. The end of the clipper era had arrived, and the day of the steamship dawned bright.

I had heard how green London town was with lovely parks dotted about. I set out to explore them at the earliest opportunity, taking in one park at a time. Above all the others, the one park I looked forward to visiting with eager anticipation was Hyde Park, about which I had read in one of my English prose selections at university, and especially, the Speakers' Corner there.

Hyde Park was not too far from my hotel by tube. The first time I went to Hyde Park, I missed the Speakers' Corner as it was farthest from the Hyde Park Corner underground station. But, I couldn't miss the highly-painted and powdered women who stood around in strategic locations beside the trees even if I wanted to. You didn't have to be told what their profession was. There was this occasion when I was hurrying towards the station one night. As I passed a large tree, a woman standing behind it said, "Hello." I stopped and enquired, "Are you looking for somebody in particular?" She was honest. "Nao, oim lookin' fer a paond." She didn't get mine. One particular woman was buxom, and she stood closest to the entrance inside the park. You couldn't help but notice her.

Each woman, apparently, would stake her claim to a particular spot which none of the others could ever occupy. I was told the story of a planter's wife who was on holiday in England. One evening, she was waiting to meet a friend somewhere near Piccadilly Circus, another place where the ladies of the night congregated, when suddenly a woman's angry voice just behind her snarled, "Get off my pitch, you bitch." The planter's wife was absolutely shattered. She narrated this incident to some of her friends when she returned from leave and the story spread.

When I eventually found the Speakers' Corner, I was utterly fascinated by it. There were those 'soap boxes' from which would-be orators would declaim passionately on subjects closest to their hearts. There was never a shortage of speakers. As soon as one speaker climbed down after having said his piece, the next one would take his place. Cars could park alongside the pavement that abutted the Corner. There was this real-life story of a man who had parked his car with the engine running near the Corner. Just then, one speaker was denouncing the Police force with great vehemence. A policeman on duty went up to the driver and said politely, "Would you mind switching off your engine, Sir, the people can't hear clearly what the gentleman is saying."

Directly across the road from the Speakers' Corner was a barbecue-kind of place, where you could actually see, standing on the pavement, choice pieces of chicken being cooked on a spit. Surprisingly, everything was very reasonably priced considering the location. You could eat a light supper of a couple of pieces of chicken and some salad – it was buffet style – and go home after listening to some interesting speeches.

One night, however, I lost track of time. When I walked back to the tube station, I found the steel gate of expanding iron at the entrance to the stairs shut and locked. I wasn't aware that the train service was terminated at a particular time at night, probably at midnight. I realized that I had to walk home. It didn't bother me too much because my own station, Gloucester Road, was just two stops away, and South Kensington, which was also fairly close to my hotel, was only one stop away. It didn't seem too far when I came to Hyde Park by train, and I knew in which direction to head back.

As I stepped onto the pavement outside, a knot of women who regularly hung out in the park came towards me. One of them was the buxom woman whom I had to pass every time I entered the park. She recognized me and smiled and wished me a cheery 'Goodnight'. They had plied their profession for the night, and were going home to rest and recoup. When I saw them in a group, I was reminded of the story of the four Oxford dons who were discussing collective nouns while on their evening stroll. A group of ladies of the night passed by, which prompted the Dean of the dons to ask his colleagues to describe them.

"A jam of tarts," said the youngest and the most impulsive of the dons.

"A flourish of strumpets," suggested the second.

"An essay of trollops, perhaps?" queried the third.

To conclude the discussion, the Dean of the dons said, "Gentlemen, I wish you would consider an anthology of pros."

Anyway, I set off on my supposedly short walk to my hotel. It was past midnight and there was a sickle-shaped moon in a clear sky. Not a single human being was in sight as I walked along, not even a policeman. Obviously, terrorism as we know it today was unheard of then, and there was no problem of security in London. I passed a cemetery and, quite unbelievably, there was a bare-branched tree with a large owl perched on one of the branches to complete the setting. As I passed, the owl hooted, leaving me to wonder whether it was a good or bad omen. All I knew was that I had to keep walking. At that time of the night, I failed to recognize any of the buildings, although I was fairly sure that I had to be somewhere in the vicinity of my hotel. There was still nobody on the streets, no traffic. I had London all to myself. It was quite uncanny. After I had wandered around aimlessly for several hours, amazingly, without feeling tired, I saw that dawn was breaking. It was a great relief. Streaks of light appeared, faintly at first and strongly afterwards. I heard the sounds of vehicles, and people started appearing. They were the milkmen on their rounds, placing bottles of milk on the doorsteps. Nobody seemed to care much about a solitary Indian man in jacket and tie wandering around. I must have been in my locality for awhile because a couple of buildings suddenly looked familiar and then, incredibly, I spotted my own hotel.

It was the height of summer in London. Depending on where I wanted to go for the evening, I would choose either the Gloucester Road or the South Kensington tube station. South Kensington station had the advantage of having a pub just outside where I'd occasionally have a drink before taking the train.

On one such evening, while I sat having a drink at the bar in the South Kensington pub, I felt somebody tap me on the shoulder. I turned round and saw a man standing behind me.

He said, "The gentleman at the corner table wants you to join their group." I looked in the direction to which he pointed. A middle-aged man smiled at me, so I went across. He made me welcome, and explained that the man who'd conveyed his invitation had been his batman during the War. My host was probably in India during the War, as many Englishmen were, but he didn't say so. On two other occasions, first when my Chairman, Col Williams, gave me lunch at his United Services Club off Trafalgar Square, and then when Mr Herbert Lloyd Pinches, a Director in the Company, took me to lunch in his Oriental Club off Oxford Street, a few men in each Club shed their traditional English reserve and came up to me, only to say that they had been in India during the War and had enjoyed their stay in my country.

I looked around at the group that I had just joined. Apart from the man who had invited me, there were two young English girls and a young West Indian man. The Englishman turned to the girls and said, "Girls, allow me to present to you the Maharaja of Cooch-Behar." One of the girls got up and came and sat in the empty chair beside me.

"Are you really the Maharaja of Cooch-Behar?" she gushed.

"Not really," I said, "I am only one of the junior ones."

She lost interest. For her, it had to be all or nothing. Soon afterwards, they were all planning to go to another pub, so I rose and left for one of my parks.

For the tennis enthusiast, the name Wimbledon means only one thing – a place of pilgrimage. My tennis-playing uncle kept a scrapbook in which the clippings of the matches played at Wimbledon were pasted in the order in which they appeared in the daily English newspaper. There were also pictures of the men and women who played at Wimbledon, complete with their names and the scores of the matches. Since I was passionately fond of tennis, I would go through the scrapbook whenever I could. I knew the names of most of the tennis players, and some of the memorable matches in which they had taken part. This was in the 1930s. There was no television in India, not even radio sets that I knew of in Trichinopoly. So, you had to depend on the written word. I didn't know anything of the other Grand Slam tennis tournaments of the day, but I knew of Wimbledon and that was sufficient for me.

In the days of the Raj, not many people I knew visited England, so you didn't even dream of being in Wimbledon at the time of the great tournament. It was nothing short of a miracle, therefore, that I found myself in London in the summer of 1957 when the Wimbledon tournament was actually taking place. I had to watch it, of course, at any cost. And, the Men's Singles Final at that, if that was at all possible.

In those days, the Men's Singles Final took place on a Saturday afternoon unlike now when it is played on a Sunday. A couple of days before the event, I dropped in casually at the office of the Tea Brokers. John Owen, the young partner whom I knew, spotted me and asked me to have lunch with him in a restaurant two days hence, on the Wimbledon Saturday. I couldn't think why he felt obliged to ask me because he and his very attractive wife, Penelope, had only sometime previously invited me to a dinner party that they had thrown for a large circle of their friends.

It was an invitation that I could not decline. I had to be at the restaurant about two hours before the scheduled start of the match. I felt reasonably certain that I could get away in time, but to make doubly certain that I would, I made it a point to mention to Owen as soon as I met him that I planned to watch the Men's Singles Final at Wimbledon immediately after lunch. He thought it was a splendid idea and asked me what I would like to drink. Thinking all the time of not delaying my exit, I asked for a small gin and tonic. Owen was the perfect host. He made small talk and brought in Wimbledon but he was obviously not a tennis buff. He didn't seem to sense my anxiety to get away early. As soon as I finished my gin, he ordered, much to my dismay, another one. Lunch was served in due course. By the time it was all over, I knew the match would have started. But it was the Final, and I believed it was quite likely to be a long-drawn-out affair.

I got to the Southfields underground station, and saw some buses waiting on the road outside to take people to the tennis courts. Some touts were also there, selling Centre Court tickets. I asked one man what a ticket would cost. He offered to sell me one for five pounds – five times the official price. (Today, a ticket to the Centre Court for the Final would cost seventy five pounds, but that is inevitable, considering the staggering amounts of prize money that the players are paid.) I asked the chap if the ticket was genuine, and how I would know if it was. He was very self-assured. He said, "Look, I'll come with you in that bus and see you through the entrance gate. Now, are you satisfied?" His demeanour was so cool that I had to be. I forked out a five-pound note and got into a bus.

As I approached the courts, I heard prolonged applause. At the entrance gate, I produced my ticket. The man there looked very carefully at the ticket first and then at me before enquiring, "Where did you get this ticket?" My heart sank. "Why, is there something wrong?" I asked. "You are lucky," he replied. "I have been turning people away who had bought old tickets from the crooks outside on the road." I heaved a sigh of relief.

While I was talking to the man at the gate, the applause appeared to be dying down and then stopped altogether. When I entered the Centre Court it was empty, quite empty. Not only was the Men's Singles Final over, I did not even get to witness the presentation ceremony at the end. The spectators were waiting for the next match to start. I was most bitterly disappointed. This was *the* Wimbledon match that I was going to watch and remember for a lifetime, and I never got to see it.

What had happened was that an Australian, Lew Hoad by name, had beaten a fellow Australian, Ashley Cooper, in three straight sets, 6-2, 6-1, 6-2 in fifty seven minutes, a record. The shortest Men's Singles Final was perhaps the match that was played in 1936 when Fred Perry beat Baron von Cramm, also in three sets, 6-1, 6-1, 6-0, in forty minutes flat. Perry, who was reputed to have 'superhuman stamina', was the last Englishman to win at Wimbledon, and he had won three consecutive finals, culminating in the match he played in 1936.

My disappointment at not being able to watch the Men's Singles Final was tempered somewhat by the fact that I was able to see the American, Althea Gibson, in action in the Mixed Doubles Final that followed. She was the first black woman to win the Women's Singles Crown a day earlier at the ripe(!), old age of thirty in quick time, beating fellow American, Darlene Hard, in straight sets, 6-3, 6-2. I had a very nice place to sit, just the second row from the sidelines, in line with the baseline. Althea Gibson was tall and well built with a deep voice to match. She struck the tennis ball very hard. She partnered Neale Fraser, an Australian. They lost to another Australian-American pair, Mervyn Rose and Darlene Hard. That same year, Althea Gibson went on to win the US Open. Just to show it was no fluke, she repeated the feat again the next year.

One could hear the partners communicating with each other quite openly, unlike today when doubles players cover their mouths when talking to each other between points so that their opponents cannot read their lips. That was the one and only time I saw live action at Wimbledon.

Even before I got to England, I had heard about Foyles. They claimed to be 'The World's Greatest Bookshop'. Being interested in books, it was the one place I just had to visit. I found the shop in Charing Cross in London, and imagined it was going to be a unique experience. In at least one way, it was. I was looking at some books on a shelf when I noticed a bespectacled man at the far end eyeing me. I thought nothing of it and moved on. As I was browsing through a book in another part of the shop, the same man appeared again and looked pointedly at me. It struck me then that I was being observed for fear that I was going to filch one of their books. It left such a bad taste in the mouth that I left the shop and never went there again.

The book section in Selfridges was, however, more enjoyable. The summer sale was on, and a large pile of books at heavily discounted prices was dumped in one room. I could browse as much as I liked without anyone watching me. One book in particular was written in a style that especially attracted me, so I bought it. The book was titled, *I Wouldn't have Missed It*, and Henry Longhurst was the author. It was mostly about his life in the Army during the Second World War and other experiences.

I mention the man's name for a special reason. A year after my visit to London, a young man called Christopher Calver (pronounced Carver) joined my Company as an Assistant. He was a Cambridge graduate, a good sportsman and his father, Alan Calver, was highly connected in the plantation circles. Calver Senior was either the Chairman or a Director of several Companies, both tea and rubber, in Africa and the Far East. Chris was engaged when he came out to Peermade, and he married a year later. His wife, Sue, was an attractive young woman, and her father was Henry Longhurst.

It wouldn't be out of place at this juncture to say something about Chris Calver himself. Christopher Calver was an enigma, at least to me. He didn't have to come out to India to start life as a lowly Assistant in a tea Company. He resigned in 1962, four years after he joined my Company. Shortly afterwards, Chris became a Director in a number of tea and rubber Companies in some African countries and in Malaysia. He then spent some years in Western Australia developing a mixed wheat, sheep and cattle farm where, sadly, at the young age of thirty five, he met his end in most tragic circumstances.

Chris Calver died of dehydration. The vehicle in which he was travelling broke down nine miles short of his destination.

The temperature in the shade was one hundred and thirty five degrees Fahrenheit, and Chris had no water. Stranded, he'd apparently decided to walk – it is the one thing I'm told that you should not do in similar circumstances. Chris collapsed and died just five hundred yards from his destination. I was privileged to write his obituary for *The Planters' Chronicle*, the magazine of UPASI, for which I had to get some details about Chris from his father. The old man was inconsolable. He said it for all of us who knew Chris when he wrote to me in one letter, "Chris was a grand chap."

∾

Death on the Estate

Richardson, my first Superintendent, was the most conscientious planter in the Company, but the least appreciated. As the junior Superintendent, Richardson always acted for the other two Superintendents, McIntyre and Horrocks, when they went on furlough. When Horrocks, the Superintendent of Ladrum Estate, went on furlough, Richardson took his place. I was then the Assistant on Ranikoil, a division of Ladrum Estate. By this time, I had been with the Company for over two years. Richardson was known to take the estate accounts to his bungalow to scrutinize them at night if he suspected that something was amiss. There nearly always was. Within a couple of months or so, Richardson suspected that some money was missing every month when the labour on Lechmi division were paid their wages. He found that a sum of exactly one thousand rupees couldn't be accounted for. He came looking for me in the field one morning, and told me about it.

Sometime earlier, somebody had told Madden that in England much time was saved when the wages of the employees were put in envelopes and handed to them at payment time each week. Madden was all ears. Here was something that he could introduce in the Company and claim another 'first'. The system was quite simple. On payment day, the Superintendent would receive a statement from the concerned division clerk which showed the amount due to each worker, and the various denominations of the total money that had to be paid. The Superintendent would then hand over the money and leave the office, returning in the evening at payment time. In the

Superintendent's absence, the division clerk with the help of the other clerks in the office would put the wages of each worker in an envelope with his or her name on it. The envelopes were then stacked neatly in the correct order on a tray. At payment time, as each name was called out by the clerk, the Superintendent (or the Assistant Superintendent on his division) would take the envelope with the money inside from the tray left by his side and hand it over to the worker. It was all very simple. A crooked mind wouldn't take too long to find ways to beat the system. The clerk on one division found one. He asked for exactly one thousand rupees more each month and adjusted the total accordingly. Undetected, the malpractice must have been going on for some time.

Richardson duly reported the discrepancy and asked for an audit of the estate accounts – one thousand rupees was a large sum of money in those days. This was acceded to, and the dates for the audit team from Madras to start work were announced. A day before the auditors were to arrive, when passing by the small well below the office, the division sweeper looked inside like he always did. He was shocked to see a number of account books floating in the water. He rushed up to the office to report what he had seen. The books were the checkrolls of the division from which the money was missing each month. The clerk had panicked, and the stupid man could only think of getting rid of the account books to escape detection. He was like the postage clerk on Kuduakarnam, only more ambitious. The man readily confessed to the crime, and expressed his desire to resign. He was only asked to pay the last thousand rupees that he had embezzled, and allowed to leave. The disgraced clerk was the brother-in-law of the Chief Clerk in the Company's Head Office. Obviously, the Management wished to avoid the publicity that this revelation would attract. The audit was aborted. Needless to say, we went back to counting out the wages for each worker in rupees and paise before handing them over like we did earlier.

Four months after I returned from my holiday in England, I got married. Life became relatively quiet, and thankfully, I didn't have to drink myself silly to retain my sanity. I returned to Kuduakarnam Estate as the Assistant there. McIntyre, my Superintendent, went on furlough prior to taking over as the General Manager of the Company from Madden, and Richardson came to act for him. One morning, I noticed a deep gash on one of his shins. The wound was still quite raw and I asked him how he came by it.

It was that time of the year when all the stores and other assets on the estate were physically checked by the Superintendent or his Assistant, if he had one. Richardson decided to take stock of the factory himself – a most onerous task. Firewood was used in the factory to fire and dry the tea in dryers. In order to pay the contractor, firewood was measured on delivery, then stacked in a firewood shed. The Tea Maker in the factory was a crook. He had got the firewood stacked all around the sides of the firewood shed, right up to the top. Only the tin roof was visible. When Richardson went to check the firewood stock, the Tea Maker told him that the firewood was tightly packed inside, and said that it would be sufficient if the outside measurements were taken – length, width and height – to calculate the cubic capacity and arrive at the total stock of firewood. Richardson didn't believe him. There was a gap on one side, so he decided to scramble up and check for himself. Sure enough, his suspicions were well founded. The middle of the shed was empty. Richardson had hurt his leg badly on a protruding piece of firewood when climbing up. The Tea Maker got away with a warning.

McIntyre was easygoing and couldn't be bothered going into the detail about anything. He would visit the factory every day for a few minutes before going home for lunch, and ask the Tea Maker the same questions in the same sequence concerning the tea being manufactured. The Tea Maker had the answers ready. He had taken the measure of his

Superintendent. There is a saying in Tamil that a thief of many days will get caught one day. That was exactly what happened to this particular man. McIntyre's successor caught him cheating in other ways and had him sacked after the mandatory domestic enquiry.

Richardson was quite unlike McIntyre. He was passionate about tea. He could talk endlessly about tea, and kept records of every field on Glenmary Estate where he was the Superintendent. His wife, on the other hand, was not one bit interested in her husband's vocation, and was generally a 'city type'. She was eventually blamed for Richardson resigning his job when he went on furlough, some months after I got married. McIntyre sent for me and told me that Richardson had resigned, and as the senior Assistant in the Company, I would be given a leg-up.

In the year 1959, six years after I had been with the Company and about a year after I got married, Horrocks, the Superintendent of Ladrum Estate, was to go on furlough, and I had to act for him. In order to be close at hand, I was transferred to Ranikoil, a division of Ladrum, a few months before I had to take charge of the estate. It was the same year that Madden was to retire and become a Director on the Company's Board. It was a case of being kicked upstairs as Madden showed no sign of wanting to leave. McIntyre was also getting old, and the Board wanted him to have the chance of being the Company's General Manager for a few years. When I congratulated Madden on his promotion as a Director of the Company, he said that he had told the Board that it wouldn't pay him to leave, and they promised to make it up to him. They did.

One Sunday morning after breakfast, I was sitting quietly at home with my wife, Susie, and our infant son, Jai, when the telephone rang. By this time, the Assistants in the Company were provided a telephone in the bungalow as one of the perks. The telephone system in Peermade at that time was not terribly sophisticated. You had an instrument but you couldn't dial the number yourself. You had to lift the receiver and wait for the operator at the manually-operated telephone exchange to come on the line. When he did, he would ask you for the number you wanted, which was either a single or a double digit as there were not too many connections then. If you were lucky, he put you through. Or else, he just said, "Unget." It may not be an English word, but its meaning was clear to everyone.

Sometimes the phone would ring, and when you picked up the receiver, there would be others already on the line. I called it the 'party line', but it was something you put up with. That Sunday morning when I picked up the receiver I heard a couple of voices on the line, voices that I instantly recognized. It was Madden talking to McIntyre, and I listened out of curiosity. The conversation went as follows:

Madden: "Mac, did you know that Davidar was elected as the Honorary Secretary of the Peermade Club at the annual general meeting last night?"

McIntyre: "No."

Madden: "Well, he was. I personally don't think that he should take up the job as he is soon to do his first real acting job. I don't think he should allow himself to be distracted but should concentrate on his acting job. What do you think?"

McIntyre: "I agree."

Madden: "In that case, shall I tell him or would you like to?"

McIntyre: "You can tell him, Charles."

Madden: "Oh, all right. Goodbye, Mac."

McIntyre: "Goodbye, Charles."

I quietly put the phone down and waited. Not surprisingly, the phone rang again soon. It was Madden as I had expected.

Madden: "Has anybody told you yet that you were elected Secretary of the Peermade Club last night?"

Me: "No, Sir." (Nobody had told me yet and I was quite literally truthful.)

Madden: "Well, you have been, and both Mr McIntyre and I agree that you shouldn't take it up when it is offered to you. You will shortly be acting for the Superintendent of Ladrum Estate and that is a big responsibility."

Me: "Okay, Sir."

Madden: "Well, that's all. Goodbye."

It was not such a big deal really, but I was relieved that I was officially saved from doing something which may have been more of a nuisance than anything else.

I enjoyed acting as the Superintendent of Ladrum, the best estate in the Company. There was more to do – the office work and correspondence such as there was, and the factory visits. And there was the additional benefit of an acting salary.

There was nothing to cause any great excitement when I started acting on Ladrum. A few months earlier, Alex York had been appointed as the new Assistant Superintendent to fill the vacancy that would arise when Madden retired. Alex, with an MA from Oxford, was the most highly qualified of the Company's Executive Staff. When Madden retired and Horrocks went on furlough, York was posted to Ranikoil division as my Assistant.

The South-West monsoon arrived late that year. Every time the monsoon was delayed, there was usually some serious problem. Soon after the monsoon broke, the rain started coming down heavily. One night in particular, it rained and rained like it had not done for many years, certainly not since I had joined the Company. The next morning, reports of heavy damage came in from the divisions. The estate roads were breached in several places and some minor bridges had been washed away. There was chaos everywhere. The labour, naturally, didn't go to work. I spent some time in the office, then decided to get back to the bungalow in the afternoon as there was nothing to do. Some time after tea, York arrived. He had bad news. He reported that one of his male workers had been washed away in the flood and the body had not been found. The placid little stream that ran through the division was in spate due to the torrential rain, and it appeared that this man had been standing on the bank. As a piece of firewood floated down, he had leaned over and tried to snatch it. He slipped and fell, and was carried away by the swirling water.

After a brief discussion, both York and I decided that we would go and inform the General Manager, McIntyre, of the mishap. McIntyre was still on Kuduakarnam, waiting for the General Manager's bungalow on Glenmary to be done up after Madden left, to suit his and his wife's tastes. Ladrum adjoined Kuduakarnam, and normally, it would not have taken much time to reach the Superintendent's bungalow by the most direct route. But the road leading there had been breached, so we were forced to turn around and take a long detour through a neighbouring estate to get to Kuduakarnam. It took us some time to get to another approach road, and when we reached the point where it led to the estate, we found that that road had also been breached. We turned around yet again and took another road, this time through Glenmary, the third estate in the Company which adjoined Kuduakarnam on the other side. An old and narrow wooden bridge stood between Glenmary and Kuduakarnam. Miraculously, it had held. By this time, darkness had fallen and a thick mist had descended. We crossed over gingerly, and when we reached the Superintendent's bungalow it was well and truly dark.

We knocked on the front door. Mrs McIntyre came to the door and seemed very surprised to see us standing there. Nobody visited the McIntyres uninvited; they kept to themselves and invitations were very rare. She asked us in and led the way to the sitting room. As we sat down, she said her husband was in the bath and would be out soon. She was all excited. Before we could explain why we had come, she blurted out, "Do you know that in last night's terrible rain Donald lost half an acre of tea when some land on the estate slid down to the bottom." York said, "Ah, that's nothing, we lost a man." It was typical of the man, he liked to say things that shocked. All that Mrs McIntyre could say was, "Oh, Oh." She kept saying 'Oh' and then lapsed into silence. Just then McIntyre walked in. We told him what had happened, and assured him that we would take the necessary action like reporting to the Police if the body was found. He approved. We left at once, declining the drink that he offered. Luckily, we reached the Ladrum bungalow safely, from where Alex made haste to get to his own bungalow.

There was no work the next day as well. The devastation was great. With some willing male workers, I got busy trying to organize some repair so that work could resume, if only slowly. Alex came to see me in the afternoon. He said the body of the man reported missing the previous day had been found, snagged in one of the bamboo clumps at the bottom of Ranikoil. Some workers had come across it when the water level had dropped. Alex asked if he could transport the body to Peermade in the estate lorry to report the incident to the Police and, if necessary, to get the post-mortem done at the Government medical facility there.

It was dark when he returned, and Alex was furious. I gave him a drink to calm him down and asked him why he was so angry. He explained that Chris Nicholl, McIntyre's Assistant on Kuduakarnam – they were good friends and still are – was visiting him, and when the lorry that was taking the body to Peermade arrived, Chris had hopped in too. At the Police Station and again at the Government dispensary, Alex said Chris got in first and reported the accident. That was what had upset him. Alex was definite that Chris had no business to act as he did and exclaimed, "After all, it was my body."

∽

The Burning Bungalow

When Horrocks returned from furlough, I was posted to Glenmary Estate as the junior Superintendent of the Company. I moved into the same bungalow in which I had lived as an Assistant when I was first taken on in 1953, except that it had been upgraded to a Superintendent's bungalow for Richardson. The bungalow now had a proper second bedroom with a modern bathroom attached, and was generally poshed up. By the end of 1960, our second child arrived, a daughter, Lulu. My wife and I had a lot to keep us occupied. At last, I was to manage my own estate. It was the oldest and lowest-yielding estate in the Company, so there was plenty of scope for improvement. And there was always something to do.

The General Manager's bungalow was located on the same estate, and following Madden's retirement, McIntyre had moved into it. True to his nature, McIntyre never interfered with the running of the estate in any way, as his predecessor liked to do. He was also not familiar with the estate as he had always been on Kuduakarnam. Occasionally, I would bump into him as he went around the estate on his motorcycle, and he would gladly accompany me to wherever I was going, exchanging pleasantries whenever we stopped to watch some work in progress.

All went reasonably well on the estate. There was no labour agitation to speak of, and life fell into a regular routine. A year later, in 1961, I went on my local leave – in July as usual – to escape the South-West monsoon which was most active at that time of the year. The South-West monsoon in Peermade had to be seen to be believed. Only God knew where all that rain came from, but it rained and rained and rained. I took my family with me, and we stayed as usual with my parents on their farm near Madras. It was good to be in the sun even if it was hot.

McIntyre was away on furlough at the time. As was customary, Horrocks stayed in his own bungalow on Ladrum while acting for McIntyre. I had been on leave only a few days, when one afternoon, while I was asleep, a telegram arrived for me. I was woken up, and couldn't believe my eyes when I read, "Your bungalow and nearly all contents destroyed by fire on Saturday night suggest you return - Horrocks." A fire? At the height of the monsoon? I got back to the estate immediately. The bungalow or what remained of it was quite a sight.

It was really amazing that a house could burn down when it was raining so heavily outside. On that fateful night, a couple of bungalow servants were in the servants' quarters, a few yards away, behind the bungalow. At about nine o'clock at night, they had smelt smoke, and went into the bungalow to investigate. They found a wooden wardrobe in the children's bedroom on fire. The general practice during the monsoon was to keep a light bulb burning in the wardrobe so that clothes and other things stored in it would not get mouldy. Although never proved, a good guess was that one of the cotton cushions that had been left in the wardrobe had fallen on top of the naked bulb and had caught fire after a while, setting the other contents alight, and eventually the wardrobe itself.

The servants had tried to put out the flaming wardrobe themselves. When their attempts failed, one of the servants rushed out in the dark and headlong down the hill on which my bungalow was situated to the nearest staff member's house to alert him. The man, Krishnan Nair, who had been a Physical Training Instructor in the Army during the Second World War, was a man of action. Krishnan Nair mustered as many men as he could at that time of the night, and sent them to the bungalow to fight the fire. He himself went to the Head Office, got it opened, and telephoned as many members of the Executive Staff as he could to get them to come if possible. Unfortunately, it was a Saturday night, and practically everybody except one man was at the Club. For some reason, Horrocks, the acting General Manager, had stayed at home, and was fast asleep in his bungalow when the phone rang. By the time Horrocks got dressed and came on the scene, the bungalow was fully ablaze. It was ironic that the man who was the first to occupy that bungalow in 1923 was also present to witness it going up in flames almost forty years later.

Telling me about the incident a few days later, Horrocks said that the burning bungalow was worth going miles to see, which in fact was what he had done. Standing helplessly outside, he saw tongues of flame racing along the recently-painted ceiling. Whoever coined the phrase, 'Got on like a house on fire' obviously knew all about it. The two rifles I owned, and a quantity of ammunition for each, were in the house at the time. Apparently, as the blaze grew ever brighter, the ammunition went off every now and then and flashed harmlessly into the night sky, providing a free fireworks display to boot. Dubious a record as it may be, I haven't heard of anybody burning his bungalow down before or since. To enable me to get back to the estate with some clothes and other necessities before I could start work again, I was given a part of the long leave I was due. I still keep the telegram as a memento.

At the end of the year, I went on long leave. Just before I got back in 1962, when I was spending the last few days of my leave in my father-in-law's place in Nagercoil, my Head Office informed me that Madden was visiting the estates as a Director, and had expressed the wish that he would like to meet me in Cochin. I was also told that a Company car would be sent to fetch me. As it happened, my return to duty coincided with Madden's date of departure for England.

Madden made desultory conversation when I met him in
Cochin. I was beginning to wonder what my roundabout trip
was all about, when, rather quickly, he came to the point.
Almost as an afterthought, he said, "Oh, and incidentally,
somebody said in Peermade that you are planning to leave
the Company. Is it true?" It was a shot in the dark. "No," I
replied. Madden knew that some years earlier, when I was a
bachelor and without any family responsibilities, I was anxious
to leave the plantations. At that time, he was equally anxious
that I stayed because it suited him and the Company. But now,
for Madden at least, I had served my purpose; my usefulness
was over. If he was disappointed with my reply, the man was
not going to give up. "I just thought I'd let you know that if
you want to leave, we won't stop you." I promised him I would
remember that. As the business for which he wanted to see
me was out of the way, he said I must be wanting to head for
the hills. The interview was over.

The reason why Madden wanted me out was not far to see.
Three Assistant Superintendents – all Englishmen – had been
with the Company for three years by then. Madden was very
happy with them, and as I saw it, in his eyes, they were ready
to take over the estates. I was in the way. If I left, as Madden
had fervently hoped I would, glory days would be back again.
All three Englishmen would soon be in charge of the
Company's estates, and for the foreseeable future at least,
everything would have been hunky-dory. The man couldn't
have had a long memory, or probably, he had conveniently
forgotten it, but one of the carrots Madden had dangled before
me in the days when I desperately wanted to leave was that if
I stayed long enough in the Company, I would have
Englishmen working under me, a signal honour.

∽

Tackling the Unions

When my bungalow burnt down, McIntyre, the General Manager was on furlough, and Horrocks was acting for him. Therefore, it fell to Horrocks to deal with all matters concerning the reconstruction of the burnt bungalow. Both of us had to go down to Cochin to meet the people who had insured the bungalow and my own personal effects, then he had to initiate correspondence to claim insurance, always keeping the Board of Directors in the picture. The Board also directed Horrocks to draw up plans urgently for another bungalow to replace the one that was destroyed. Much time was lost because of the differences between the Board and Horrocks about how the new bungalow should be built. Horrocks sought professional help in designing the bungalow, while the Board wanted the Executives in the Company to forward plans to them for their approval. When the Board went into the details, inevitably, they raised all kinds of objections. I remember one Executive had designed a bungalow with the dining room right in front. The Board commented that by the time the soup reached the dining room from the kitchen it would have become cold! There were no computers or e-mail then, so letters and plans went back and forth at a snail's pace for the next three months or so until it was time for McIntyre to return from furlough.

Horrocks was retiring and leaving Peermade for good in a year's time, so he had also to plan his own departure. It meant selling those possessions that he didn't want to take back with him and issuing receipts for the items sold. He then had to apply to the Reserve Bank of India for permission to repatriate the money thus received. In a way, it was unfair for an expatriate leaving India after a lifetime of service – Horrocks had been with the Company for thirty nine years – to continue to manage his estate and prepare to retire as well. It could not have been easy especially since the man was single and had to do everything himself.

I have mentioned all this because Horrocks couldn't spend much time effectively supervising the work on the divisions. Ladrum was the best estate in the Company, but not without problems. Ranikoil division always had troublesome labour, but one of the other divisions, Lechmi, saw a steady rise in labour union activity which the subordinate staff on the division found impossible to control. The leaders of the established labour unions were always looking for opportunities to create trouble as that ensured their own survival. They were probing all the time, and pounced on any perceived weakness of the management to pursue their own nefarious ends. They had all the help and cooperation they needed from some of the disgruntled workers, who basked in the prominence they got by serving on the committees that the union leaders set up on the estate.

The staff on Lechmi couldn't stand up to the union activity which was making rapid inroads into the normal work on the division. So, even though I was taking over a very good estate from Horrocks at the end of 1962, there was much strife to contend with. I liked to be in the field for much of the morning where the tea was said to be made, but increasingly, I found myself spending a lot of my time on Lechmi. At midday, the pluckers were weighed up at convenient spots in the fields, from where the leaf they'd plucked was transported to the factory. On one occasion, I saw a male worker standing by the side of the Plucking Writer as he was weighing up the leaf. I asked him what he was doing there. He said he was checking the correctness of the weight of the leaf that the Plucking Writer was calling out for each plucker. It turned out that he was the union representative on the division. He said that he had been authorized by the union to be at the weighing spots to monitor the Plucking Writer's work. I told him quietly to go and do the work that he was allotted, and said that I would oversee the work on the division. He didn't like being ticked off in front of the other workers in whose eyes he wanted to appear important. He left the scene with bad grace. I made a mental note of the man. It was not unusual for the troublemakers to step out of line sooner or later and court dismissal. If one of the union office-bearers was sacked, much labour unrest generally ensued because of the position he or she occupied. It sorely tested one's patience before the much-awaited opportunity presented itself. I remember Horrocks telling me once that he had asked the Conductor on a division to deal with a troublemaker. The Conductor, a wise man, counselled patience. He was not going to rush into any situation. He told the Superintendent to leave the matter to him and said that one day he would get the man, "Slowly, slowly like catching monkey." So, I remembered the Conductor's words and waited for the right time to come.

All in all, it was not a happy situation. To complicate matters, China attacked India unexpectedly in October 1962 in the region known as NEFA (North Eastern Frontier Agency) which acquired the name Arunachal Pradesh in 1972 when it became a Union Territory. I wrote to the Army Headquarters volunteering my services for the country, and was not altogether surprised when there was no reply. After all, I had been out of the Army for ten years.

At the estate level, we started collecting money from the labour and staff to forward to the National Fund that had been set up to cope with the emergency. The labour union was affiliated to the Congress party, the party in power. The Secretary of the labour union also went about asking for contributions from the labour which hampered our own efforts to raise funds. He had been the cause of all the labour trouble we were having on Lechmi, and was increasingly becoming a nuisance in this area of activity as well. I thought that if I complained to the authorities about the confusion that was being created, the man's activities on the estate would somehow be checked. In my enthusiasm, however, I marked copies of my letter to a number of important people in governmental authority including the Prime Minister.

The union leader managed to get hold of a copy of my letter. He wrote to me saying I had defamed him, and that unless I apologized to him unconditionally, and in writing, he would initiate legal proceedings against me in a court of law. I told my General Manager about the union leader's letter. He asked me to consult with the Company's legal adviser who lived fifty miles away in Kottayam, in case the situation turned out to be serious. When I went to see him, the legal adviser was quite cross with me. He said that since I had mentioned the man by name, and had sent copies of my letter to all kinds of dignitaries, I had indeed committed libel, and had laid myself open to the charge of defamation of a man's character. He advised that I must mollify the man without actually grovelling in the dust. He set out to draft a letter, after consulting the dictionary several times for the correct meanings of words. The final effort turned out to be a masterpiece in prevarication. He said, in effect, that if I had offended the man, then I was sorry, no more.

I was seeing the union Secretary much of the time in the office of the Deputy Labour Officer stationed in Peermade. The unions harassed the management in several ways. One tactic was to constantly make all kinds of demands in writing. Copies of the letters concerning the issues raised were sent to the Deputy Labour Officer, who in turn, would immediately convene conciliation conferences to try and arrive at some sort of settlement. There was never any end to these conferences as it was impossible to concede to their every demand. The Company's legal adviser – the same person who drafted my letter to the union leader – would sometimes attend the conciliation conferences on request. When any serious issues which involved a legal overtone arose, he would always affirm, "We agree to disagree." At one of these conferences, the union man complained to the Labour Officer that I had been devious in my letter to him, and that I must apologize in straightforward terms. In some situations, as in this one, silence is the best reply. So, I kept mum. The man gave up after some time in sheer disgust. He must have realized that as a Company we had greater resources than he himself could muster if he had to initiate legal proceedings against me.

Meanwhile, the pinpricks continued. There could be no satisfactory settlement to the disputes that the union man was bringing up all the time, and I was wasting much valuable time in the office of the Labour Officer. The union resorted to doing everything they possibly could to try and humiliate me to achieve their ends. Before every conference, the union leaders on the division would hold a meeting to discuss the strategy they should adopt. The Conductor would have a mole attending these meetings, and he would pretend to be a good friend of the union chaps. Later, the Conductor would send me a detailed report on their deliberations. The main stratagem they had agreed upon was to do things to annoy me at these conferences, and to make me feel small. They believed it would make me feel most uncomfortable if some of my own workers sat near me at the conferences and smoked cigarettes, blowing the smoke around me. The Labour Officer seemed powerless to stop this nonsense. Two chaps would sit on either side of me and pass each other a packet of cigarettes in front of me, light up, then blow the smoke everywhere except in my face. One of the chaps who usually sat next to me was the same fellow whom I had ticked off in the field when I first saw him checking the pluckers' leaf weighments. I bided my time knowing it had to come sooner or later. And, it did.

The estate worker in question was also the Convenor of the union Committee on the division. He got bolder as time went by, thinking that nobody could touch him. Eventually, he committed a gross act of misconduct. I was waiting for him to do just that. I promptly charge-sheeted him, conducted a domestic enquiry and dismissed him from service. Naturally, all hell broke loose. It was now a question of riding out the storm.

The sacking of the union man helped in other ways. The labour on the division had obviously been watching to see how the management was going to deal with the union. With the man they had been afraid of out of the way, they started responding positively. There was a distinctly palpable improvement in the labour situation on the division.

The Secretary of the union now had to deal with the consequences arising out of the dismissal of his right-hand man, apart from pursuing the dozens of demands that he had previously raised which were pending resolution. One of them was especially tricky. I had arranged for plucking to be done *on contract* on some Sundays which was against the law. I would have been in serious difficulty if he had insisted on the law being honoured. Another was settling the affairs of the dismissed man, who, luckily for me, he did not qualify for gratuity as his service on the estate fell short by a few months. The Secretary had to pacify him somehow, if not to get him reinstated, then to at least recover his gratuity for the years he'd worked. In my Company, unlike in some others, when a man got sacked, he stayed sacked. I least expected that the dismissed man himself would eat humble pie. On several afternoons, I would see him standing outside my office window, generally appearing most penitent. He would wish me if I looked in his direction and smile in a sickly fashion.

The union Secretary, for once, sought a compromise. His man was obviously pushing him. He indicated to me that he would be willing to drop many of his demands if I agreed to pay the dismissed worker gratuity for his period of service. I kept him waiting for some time, then told him I might consider his request if he dropped *all* his pending demands. Predictably, he replied that he would retract his stand on all issues except the one relating to Sunday plucking, knowing that he was on solid ground there. Sensing that he was weakening, I could afford to refuse to budge. He finally gave in. I got him to *officially* withdraw *all* the demands over which a lot of my time had been wasted thus far, and paid the man who was sacked his gratuity. There was a measure of peace after that. We could get on with our normal work on the division, something that had been difficult to achieve for a long period of time. Once a labour union has been allowed to become powerful on the estate, it is not easy to regain control.

Sita, the main division on the estate, had remained relatively trouble-free. The Conductor on the division was the senior man who knew how to 'catch monkeys'. Even he was to have big trouble, trouble that I had quite stupidly caused. It came about this way.

By prior arrangement, I had to leave the office one afternoon to hold discussions about some important work that was being carried out on the estate. When I came out, a man whom I did not recognize was standing by the side of my motorcycle on the office verandah. He just said that I must arrange to supply weather protectives that year for the workers. I did not know that he was the union representative on the division. According to the law, estate managements had to supply two coarse blankets or *cumblies* to every worker, meant as weather protectives against the prolonged wet weather that we experienced every year. By common consent, the estates generally gave an agreed amount in cash in lieu of the physical supply of blankets. As long as there was no trouble, the Government labour department took no notice of this arrangement.

We had already paid out the money and all the labour had accepted it, so the man's demand took me by surprise. I could have been tactful and asked him to come another time when we could talk as I had to attend to another important engagement just then. Instead, I was abrupt and told him that the workers had accepted the cash we'd paid, and that if he arranged for the money to be returned, then we would consider the supply of blankets. Having said that, I got on my bike and rode off without giving the incident another thought. After all, he was only one man making the demand, and there was nobody else around. I never dreamt that a nasty situation would arise because of my impetuosity.

I was astounded, therefore, when an official demand for *cumblies* was made by the Secretary of the labour union. When the labour union wanted a major demand to be met, they would add several others to the list. When a settlement was eventually arrived at, both sides would claim victory. The management would declare that of the dozen or so demands that the union raised, they had given into only three or four when originally there had been only one; the union, on the other hand, would assert that they got the management to agree to several when they had made only one demand in the beginning.

As no agreement was immediately possible on the *cumbly* front, trouble erupted on the division in a big way. Not only was normal work badly affected, but ugly demonstrations also took place every day. Several workers, mainly women, would march up to my bungalow after work and stand outside the gate, shouting slogans and abusing me. The agitation took place during the monsoon, yet they came up every single day, even when it was raining heavily. Not even the rain deterred them.

The labour unrest gathered momentum. One day I was returning late in the evening from Kottayam where I had gone to consult the Company's lawyers about how to deal with the agitation. As I neared the bungalow, a number of pluckers were coming down from the bungalow gate to go to their living quarters. When I entered the house, I found my wife, Susie, in a filthy temper. She said to me that if she knew how to use my gun, she'd have taken a shot at all those women who stood outside the gate shouting and screaming at the top of their voices for what seemed to her an eternity. She would have done it too. Susie was generally placid by temperament and gentle by nature, and she was relatively small-made too. But when provoked she became like a garden shrew which, ounce for ounce, is reputed to be the fiercest living creature on earth. I say this because she had demonstrated on at least one occasion an act of daring which you wouldn't normally associate with a woman.

Susie was returning to Peermade from Nagercoil where she had gone to spend some time with her parents. I had sent a car down with a driver to fetch her. Night had fallen when they were still some distance from home, and a heavy mist had blanketed the whole area. I know nothing about the proverbial London pea-souper, but the mist that covered Peermade after a spell of rain could run it close for blanking out visibility. Inching its way forward, the car reached Stagbrook, which was only a few miles from Glenmary where we lived. Suddenly a jeep appeared from the opposite direction and rammed into the car. The two machines had somehow got their bumpers interlocked, and neither could move in any direction. Our driver told my wife that he would ring and inform me about the incident from a shop nearby which he knew had a telephone. He asked her to remain in the car until he got back, and left the headlights on. My wife who was sitting in the back seat could see two men talking to each other in the jeep. When they saw the driver leaving the car and going away, the men thought the car was empty. They got down from the jeep and tried to extricate their vehicle to make good their escape when they could. Susie realized what the two chaps were up to. She jumped out of the car and caught one of them by his shirt collar and told them they were not leaving until her own driver returned. She then ordered them to get back into the jeep. The fellows hadn't expected this sudden turn of events and meekly obeyed. They sat in the jeep until our driver returned after receiving instructions from me. To say the least, foolhardy though Susie's action was, it worked. I do not believe that any other woman in her place would have had the guts to tackle those two men alone that night as she had done.

The union employed all manner of tactics to unsettle you during the labour agitations. One of them was to install loudspeakers at strategic locations in such way that you could hear the speeches that were broadcast over them. Inflammatory speeches were made both in the morning and in the evening by the union office-bearers and representatives of the union on the division. In one such speech, the union man attacked me personally in vile terms. While I did not get to hear it myself, the Conductor who did sent me a written report mentioning some of the nasty things that had been said about me. It was unpleasant. I sent the report to the Company's lawyers and asked if some appropriate legal action could be instituted against the man. In their reply the lawyers said that while some of the remarks – assuming that the report was accurate – appeared to be defamatory, I was at a disadvantage as there was nothing in black and white. They went on to say that slander, which was spoken defamation, unlike libel which was written defamation, was extremely difficult to prove in a court of law – no two witnesses were likely to agree on the exact words spoken, and several witnesses could be produced to swear that something else had been said instead. 'Let sleeping dogs lie' was their considered advice.

It was a long time before the dispute could be settled by the Labour department, and much avoidable unhappiness was caused in the meantime. The Roman poet, Publius Papinius Statius, who lived in the first century AD, was a wise man. In those ancient days he counselled, "Give no reins to your inflamed passions, take time and a little delay. Impetuosity manages all things badly." Indeed. In hindsight, I believe, if I had taken a little time and not been impetuous, things could have been managed more felicitously.

While the Sita and Lechmi divisions eventually came under reasonable control, Ranikoil continued to simmer. When Horrocks retired, an Indian, a Punjabi, was taken on and posted as my Assistant on Ranikoil. About the same time, another Indian Assistant was also hired and posted to Kuduakarnam. These were the first Indians to be employed in SITE after I was engaged nine years earlier. My Punjabi Assistant didn't speak Tamil, the language of the workers, and didn't make an effort to learn it either. He was also rash in making the observation that in order to run the estate it was not necessary to know the local language. Like so many other things, this bit of indiscretion on the part of my Assistant also reached the ears of the Board and led to his eventual downfall.

The Conductor who served under me several years earlier was now in charge of Lechmi and a new Conductor took his place on Ranikoil. The previous Conductor on Ranikoil lived in constant fear. He felt that the workers whom he had antagonized would harm him physically. I remember once when I came back from leave, I saw the man walking around the division with two men, one of them walking a few paces ahead of him and another a few paces behind him, both armed with heavy lathis. I asked him what it was all about. He told me that serious threats of violence were held out against him, and that the two men were his bodyguards. I told him it was the surest way of asking for trouble, and said that if the threats the rowdy elements were putting out against me had come true, I myself should have been badly damaged by now. I instructed him to give up his bodyguards forthwith. He did so reluctantly, and I was very relieved that no physical harm came to him as long as he was on the division.

Actually, I doubt that anybody was ever completely free from fear. Even if you were afraid, and there were many situations on the estate when you had real cause to feel fear especially in times of labour trouble, you had to put on a bold front outwardly and, surprisingly, no harm befell you. The great American tank commander of World War II fame, General George S Patton, who seemed to be such a fearless individual said, "Courage is fear holding on a minute longer."

The new Conductor on Ranikoil was brash. Apparently, he was always taunting the troublemakers on the division that they couldn't frighten him, and that he knew how to deal with them. Unnecessarily, he was asking for trouble.

One day I was at the office of the District Labour Officer in Kottayam attending an important conference relating to the problems on Ranikoil as they could not be resolved at the level of the Labour Officer in Peermade. They were very tricky issues, and the Committee of my District Planters' Association was of the view that since I was having a difficult time, the Secretary of the State Planters' Association should assist me in the negotiations that were taking place. As desired by my Committee, I met the Secretary on my way to the office of the District Labour Officer, showed him the demands made by the labour union, and explained the stage at which matters stood. He read them and said, quite bluntly, that he didn't think a settlement could be negotiated. But he was willing to come along and hold my hand if I was that keen. I told him it was my Committee's wish, not mine. He agreed.

Before going to the office of the Labour Officer, I stopped by the Company's legal advisers, a very respectable firm with much local influence, to consult with them as they had been in on the matter so far. I also asked if one of their men, a senior advocate and a good personal friend, would be free to come to the conference with me for a while. I felt that his very presence would make a significant difference to the outcome of the negotiations. The senior partner of the firm saw the Secretary of the Planters' Association hanging about. He took me aside and asked if he was coming too. I had not reckoned with the possibility that the Secretary and our legal advisers, all local men, would not get on. I told the partner that he was. In that case, he declared emphatically, their own man would not accompany me. I preferred the lawyer to the Secretary and told him so. I also offered to undertake the delicate task of telling the Secretary that he could return to his own office. When I gave the man the news that I thought he would not take too well, he actually seemed very relieved and left quickly.

The lawyer who came with me had a quiet chat with the District Labour Officer, pointing out to him some aspects of the law that must be borne in mind while conducting the conference. The Labour Officer listened without saying anything. To my utter surprise, my lawyer friend thereafter wished the Labour Officer well and left.

After some time, the Secretary of the labour union arrived and the conference began. We were making no headway, and the atmosphere that prevailed seemed to suggest another deadlock. Just when everything seemed hopeless, my Assistant on Ranikoil walked in. He said to me quite loudly – so that everyone present could hear – that his Conductor had been badly beaten up by some workers in the division. He also informed me that he had brought the injured man in his car and had admitted him in the District Hospital in Kottayam after having reported the matter to the Police.

I told the District Labour Officer that the meeting could not go on as I was leaving immediately for the hospital to see my man. Filled with indignation, I added that for all I cared, the union could go to hell. The union man had not bargained for this development. He was speechless.

My Assistant and I proceeded to the hospital where the Conductor was lying on a bed, heavily bandaged, in a very crowded ward. He could speak to me, however, and related what had happened. I could see that he had been asking for trouble as I had apprehended earlier.

Anyway, we returned to the estate feeling very subdued. In due course, the District Labour Officer posted another conference to discuss the pending issues. He had probably appealed to the union man to be more reasonable, and to cooperate this time around. To everyone's surprise, the meeting went smoothly and we did reach a settlement on the issues that had defied a solution for a long time.

While we waited for the settlement that had been agreed upon to be typed out for our signatures to be appended to it, I congratulated the District Labour Officer for having resolved such difficult issues satisfactorily. I told him it must be a feather in his cap. The man had a sense of humour. He said that he didn't wear caps.

Even one rowdy in the workforce could spell trouble. The man would always be looking for a chance to stir things up, if only to seemingly elevate his status on the division. My Punjabi Assistant on Ranikoil was succeeded by a young Malayalee. My new Assistant wasn't on the division long when one of the old troublemakers got up to mischief once again. He was charge-sheeted for a misconduct that he had committed, and the charge, a serious one, was conclusively proved. He had to be dismissed. Trouble again.

The workers, as expected, started shouting slogans every day just outside the bungalow of the Assistant, much to the annoyance of his newly-married wife. As the Superintendent of Ladrum Estate, initially, I was left alone. The conciliatory conferences met with the usual intransigent attitude of the union. They wanted the dismissed worker to be reinstated, but in accordance with the Company policy, we declined to oblige.

Meanwhile, the General Manager proceeded on furlough. As the senior Superintendent in the Company, the No.2, the Board asked me to move into the General Manager's bungalow on Glenmary Estate and run the Company from the Head Office there rather than from my own estate as was the practice earlier. When the worker was sacked, I was the Superintendent of Ladrum. Now I was the acting General Manager. The union decided, therefore, to concentrate on harassing me. They declared that until the dismissed man was given back his job, they would go on a hunger strike. A tarpaulin shelter was put up just outside my bungalow gate, and two or three chaps sat in it day and night. None of the hunger strikers seemed the worse for wear even after several days of 'going without food'. It was all a joke. It was said that the men who were supposed to be on hunger strike were fed at night when everyone was asleep, and no one was looking. While the slogan-shouting went on morning and night, the crowds outside the gate in the evenings were larger and more vociferous, and the abuse against me rather colourful.

My wife and children were in Madras at the time. Susie, a former educationist, was keen that she should be with the children when they started school, so they lived in a rented flat there. When they came to be with me for the Christmas holidays, the demonstration was still very much on. We could hear what was being shouted clearly, as the sitting room windows faced the gate and were not too far from it.

After my family joined me, the shouting got even louder. Among other choice names for me, one evening they called me a *kaandaa mirugam* (rhinoceros). My son, Jai, who was about eight years old then, kept looking at me closely and said to his mother that his father didn't look like a *kaandaa mirugam*. Jai certainly knew how a rhinoceros looked. When he was a little boy of about six or seven years, I went to Madras on leave to be with them. One day, we went as a family to see the film *Hatari* in a small cinema in Madras. *Hatari*, starring that rugged and lovable actor John Wayne, was shot in 1962 in Tanzania, the largest country in Eastern Africa – larger than Kenya and Uganda put together. The film was all about wild animals for which Tanzania was, and still is, famous. The two rhinoceros chases in the film were the most thrilling. Every time the rhinoceros appeared on the screen, and especially when it charged head-on, Jai felt the need to visit the toilet and I had to accompany him. I remember we made several trips.

The demonstrations continued even after my family returned to Madras at the end of the school holidays. They were stepped up on Sundays. You really had to admire the way they were organized. From the various divisions in the Company where this particular union was in some strength, batches would come over in waves on Sundays to shout and scream throughout the morning. It didn't bother me too much, though. I was a grass widower, and I generally spent the day at the Club. However, the threats of physical violence against me continued.

One Sunday, I stayed in the Club longer than usual with some friends. For some reason, we didn't disperse until quite late that night. At the entrance to the estate where I lived, there was a gate which was kept locked. When anyone wanted to enter the estate in a vehicle, the watchman would come out from his hut and open it. Just beyond the gate, the road curved a little and began to rise. You had to slow down and change gears before gathering speed.

That night, as I went through the gate and was taking the curve slowly as usual, the headlights of the car picked out a man sitting below a culvert just by the side of the road – an ideal site for an ambush. Still driving very slowly, more by instinct than by intention, I stopped as I came abreast of the man. I could see one or two other chaps with him. Mustering up the courage needed, I asked the man what they were doing in a voice that I hoped didn't quaver. He said, to my vast relief, that they were trying to flush out a porcupine that had run inside the culvert. I was almost sure they were waiting to get me.

When the General Manager returned, I was able to get back to Ladrum. The agitation continued and protracted negotiations with the Deputy Labour Officer made scant headway. Eventually it ended as it always did, with a bit of give and take, usually when both the parties to the dispute got tired.

Ladrum was a good place, in spite of the difficulties that I had to face when taking over the estate. The tea was younger than on the other two estates in the Company, and more often than not, the result of any good work was tangible. After all the unpleasantness that one had to put up with during a labour agitation, at the end of it all, you had to live with the labour and it was wise not to bear a grudge. Those were the sagacious words uttered by a senior British planter in another Company who had to bear much harassment himself.

The workers who gave me the most trouble could also show much magnanimity on occasion. I experienced one such gesture on the eve of my departure for Glenmary to assume charge of the Company. On the last Sunday that my wife and I spent on Ladrum, we heard several people coming up to the bungalow, and went out onto the verandah to investigate. A large number of workers from the Sita division, mostly women, were streaming into the bungalow compound dressed in their Sunday best. I was astonished. The woman representative of the union who had given me a lot of trouble over the *cumbly* issue led the way. During the agitation, rain or shine, she would head the procession of women who assembled at the bungalow gate, and shout uncomplimentary slogans for the others to repeat after her. That Sunday, they had come to bid farewell to my wife and me, and to wish us well in our new assignment. All was forgiven, all was forgotten. I was deeply touched.

Ascending the Gaddi

I ascended the 'gaddi' in April 1969, almost sixteen years to the day after I joined the Company. I very nearly didn't.

My predecessor handed his letter of resignation to a visiting Director at the end of 1968. At the same time, he took it upon himself to tell the Director what the Company's future set-up should be. From what happened shortly afterwards, it appeared that the Director had apparently not only accepted the departing General Manager's gratuitous advice but had also forwarded it to the Company's Chairman in England, recommending that it be accepted. Things moved rather swiftly thereafter.

Around Christmas 1968, a letter arrived from the Company's Secretaries, detailing the disposition of the Executive Staff following the departure of my predecessor. I was surprised to see that I had been designated not only as the General Manager of the Company, but also as the Superintendent of Glenmary Estate on which the Company's Head Office and the General Manager's bungalow were situated. My predecessor had deliberately wanted to devalue the top job knowing that I was going to succeed him. He was very pleased to have pulled it off, and told whoever cared to listen – and there were some who were curious to know what would happen – that Davidar would hold both positions in the Company. When the orders were made public, he was filled with glee that his advice had been heeded. He actually had the nerve to tell me that there was not enough work to do as the Company's General Manager. If the man chose not to exert himself – and ennui can kill – it did not mean that there was no work for the number one of a plantations company.

In fact, I had more work than any of my predecessors because of changing circumstances. I had inexperienced men working under me who had been promoted as acting Superintendents of estates. One of them would just sign the letters that his smart-alec Head Clerk put in front of him. The rupeeisation of the Company was also being contemplated. The Foreign Exchange Regulation Act (FERA) promulgated by the Government required a certain percentage of the equity of foreign companies to be in Indian hands. In order to comply with the FERA regulations, I had to enter into correspondence of the kind never before attempted, meet all kinds of people and undertake a lot of travel. It was strange that Madden, one of the Directors on the Company's Board, had acquiesced to the revised management structure. He had himself been a General Manager for seven years (in less stressful times), and knew the responsibilities that went with the job. After Madden, there were two other General Managers (including the man who was leaving), and, oddly enough, it hadn't occurred to anyone that the Company's General Manager had very little work to do, if indeed that was true.

The Director who had forwarded my predecessor's resignation letter and also his recommendations for acceptance, was still in the district when the Board's orders were received. He was visiting the estates of another Company being their Director as well. I managed to contact him, and made it plain that I was unhappy doing two jobs in the Company. I requested his permission to write to the Board and apprise them of my concerns. He agreed.

I wrote a fairly long official letter to the Chairman voicing my apprehensions. I knew from personal experience that the Chairman, Col Williams, was a very just man and that my case would receive a fair hearing. I merely said in my letter to him, that it would be tactically unwise from the Company's point of view for me to work as the General Manager, and also carry out the duties of the Superintendent of Glenmary Estate at the same time, and provided valid reasons to substantiate my sense of disquiet. While I had made no threat, I was clear in my own mind that if the Board had insisted that their original order should stand, I would leave. I didn't know what I would do had that came about, but I knew there could not be a compromise when it was a question of self-respect.

The Chairman's decision which was not long in coming was typical of the man. He had sized up the situation immediately, and the Board's earlier decision was reversed, much to the discomfiture of my predecessor whose ploy hadn't succeeded. I was not entirely surprised, therefore, when the Secretaries wrote another letter soon afterwards appointing me solely as the Company's General Manager in India – the official designation. Two Assistants with just about five years' experience each were promoted as acting Superintendents of the two estates in which the vacancies had arisen.

In a private and confidential letter that he wrote to me at the same time, Col Williams said that I had a difficult job in front of me, and it would not be mine if the Board had felt that I was not up to it. And, he added, "We all wish you the best of luck and we hope that if you have any problems which are worrying you, you will not hesitate to seek our assistance."

Interestingly, before my predecessor was handed over charge of the Company, my own name had been proposed in an unlikely fashion. It was common practice among the Superintendents in my Company to go to the estate office first thing in the morning, attend to whatever needed to be dealt with, then return to the bungalow for breakfast before setting out to the field. I was a Superintendent at the time, and followed the established routine.

One morning, just as we finished breakfast, Horrocks rode up on his bike. He told my wife and me that he was coming straight from the Head Office where he had just met McIntyre, the General Manager. McIntyre was retiring in a few months' time and his successor had not yet been named. The Board was taking quite a bit of time to announce its decision. My predecessor was only a few months senior to me, and we had both been in the Company for about ten years. There was much speculation about who would succeed McIntyre. It was even rumoured that an outsider with more planting experience than my predecessor might be appointed as the Company's new General Manager. Under normal circumstances, Horrocks, the senior Superintendent, would have been the automatic choice for the job, but he had earlier announced that he was not in the race.

Both my predecessor and I had worked under Horrocks on Ladrum for varying periods. Horrocks had suggested to McIntyre that my name could be put forward to the Board to take over his, McIntyre's, job. McIntyre had told him firmly that ours was a sterling Company, and no Indian could ever become its General Manager. If Horrocks hadn't told us about his conversation with McIntyre, this revelation would have never come to light. I told him I didn't want the job. He asked, jokingly, if I thought that an international situation would arise if his recommendation was accepted.

About three months after I had assumed charge of the Company, Chris Nicholl, the last European in the Company, went on furlough to England and resigned. It was bruited about that he left the Company because he didn't want to work under an Indian. Chris Nicholl and I were very good friends, and we still very much are. As he and I have never spoken about it, I have no idea if there was any truth to the rumour at all.

When Nicholl resigned, yet another Assistant, with even less service than the other two who had been made acting Superintendents, took his place until a new senior Superintendent was appointed to replace him. Thus, I had three Assistants acting as Superintendents when I became the Company's General Manager. Yet another record, albeit a dubious one.

I was in the saddle for only a few months when the Chairman, Col Williams, came on an official visit, his last to the Company's estates although I didn't know it at the time. At the end of his visit, he was to interview some men in Cochin who had applied for the senior Superintendent's job in the Company. There was one Englishman among them whom the Chairman seemed to favour, although he thought quite well of an Indian too. He told me afterwards that he had made it a point to mention to the Englishman that if selected, he'd have to work under an Indian. So, there was some genuine prejudice among the Europeans about having to work under an Indian. The man in question had been a planter in India for some years, and had apparently assured Col Williams that he didn't think it would be a problem.

Before they left for Home, it was usual for visiting Directors to meet the heads of the various organizations in Cochin with whom we had business dealings. In most cases, the General Manager accompanied them, and this time, I was with the Chairman. A European agency based in Cochin supplied factory machinery, and we had placed an order with them for the supply of an important machine for one of our factories. The agency was taking a long time to execute the order. Col Williams, who was aware of the situation, asked me to arrange a meeting with the No.1 of that firm, an Englishman, to discuss the matter with him.

On our way to the agency house, I gave the Chairman the file containing the correspondence from the time the order was placed. He went through it and told me that everything was now clear to him. When we were ushered into the office of the No.1, he greeted the Chairman and barely acknowledged my presence.

The Chairman briefed the man about the nature of our visit. Suddenly and quite unexpectedly, Col Williams said that the General Manager would explain the problem in detail. The Englishman winced noticeably. When I laid bare the facts of the matter, he addressed his comments to the Chairman, calling him 'Colonel' all the time. He hardly ever looked at me. He obviously subscribed to the McIntyre school of thought even if the glowering portrait of Winston Churchill didn't hang above his head. He promised my Chairman that he would look into the matter, and would do what he could to expedite the dispatch of the machine we'd ordered. The interview ended and we left the man's office. When we came out, Col Williams declared that he didn't like the man. I knew what he meant. That particular Englishman should have considered himself lucky that more than two decades after the country had become independent, he could continue to be arrogant while enjoying the comfortable life that the country offered him. He was probably one of the few exceptions, as I had a very good relationship with his successor.

To be fair, some Indians also thought that I didn't rightfully deserve the honour of heading a sterling company. After I took over as the General Manager, I met the No.1 of the tea broking firm whom we dealt with. He asked me, quite seriously, "Who else have they got?" He would have preferred to deal with a white man, *any white man,* to a black man. And this man claimed to be a good friend of mine. A fair weather friend I was to discover. When I retired and went to live in The Nilgiris, I was at the wedding reception of the daughter of a planter in the Coonoor Club. This man was also there. We saw each other at very close quarters but he didn't show the slightest sign of recognition.

It was very important that a rapport was established between the Chairman and the Board of the Company on the one hand, and their Chief Executive who looked after the Company's affairs five thousand miles away on the other. I was lucky to have had Col Williams as the Chairman when I took charge of the Company. I had known him for about fourteen years by then, ever since I was an Assistant Superintendent. I also knew his family as I was invited to spend a weekend with them on my first visit to England in 1957.

On his last visit, as we sat and chatted before dinner one evening, my Chairman told me a story, apropos nothing in particular. He said there was this riot in Poona during the days of the Raj. The Viceroy, an immensely powerful man, sent for the Commander-in-Chief (C-in-C) as he was very concerned that the riot had not been checked.

The Viceroy said to the C-in-C, "Bob, the Poona riot has been going on for some time as you know, and I wonder what you are doing about it?"

"Nothing."

"Oh, and why not, Bob?"

"I have a man on the spot dealing with it. He is doing a reasonably good job and if I think that he cannot cope, then I'll intervene."

"Oh, it's all right then, I understand."

In his own inimitable style, Col Williams was telling me indirectly that I enjoyed his confidence, and that he would not interfere with the way I went about the job I was doing unless he had to.

∾

Impending Change

E arly in 1972, Col Williams, the Chairman, wrote me a letter suggesting that it would be expedient if I could visit England in the summer of that year in order to hold detailed discussions with all the Directors of the Board on outstanding issues. This seemed to be the only feasible option as otherwise I had occasion to bring up Company matters with only one Director at a time when he visited the Company's estates each year.

Accordingly, I went to England in July that year, and a whole range of issues was discussed at length and many important decisions were taken. The youngest Director, who was about my age, said in a letter to me that he found my visit a 'great success'. (I shall refer to him as John as he insisted that I call him by his first name.) He was of the view that it would help the Board considerably to have these discussions every year. That may not have been his personal opinion alone, as the Chairman wrote me later that year saying that he believed mention was made of the policy for my future visits to the United Kingdom. In actual fact, nobody told me of this policy if there was indeed one.

In November that year, I received a letter from the Chairman in which he said that my long leave was due the following year in summer. He asked if I could visit England again, and suggested that my wife, Susie, accompany me.

All the Directors acknowledged my wife's unobtrusive contribution behind the scenes. My Chairman especially took a great liking to her. He said to me when I saw him off at the airport at the end of his last visit that he was all admiration for the way Susie looked after him during his stay with us. My wife read voraciously, wrote brilliantly and could engage the Directors in conversation on many subjects as she was an eclectic. She kept two or three diaries simultaneously in which she meticulously recorded her observations. When I was the Superintendent of Ladrum Estate, Michael Jackson, the then Manager-in-India of the other sterling Company in the district, was appointed the Visiting Agent of my Company. Jackson's maternal uncle was Field Marshal Sir Claude Auchinleck – The Auk to those who knew him – who retired in 1947 as Commander-in-Chief in India after forty three years of distinguished military service. Jackson was the acknowledged local expert birdwatcher. On one of his visits to my estate, Susie and he were engrossed in an animated discussion on the migratory habits of mynahs. When he wrote to thank her for her hospitality, he made it a point to mention that it was very rare for him to come across a planter's wife who was so knowledgeable about birds.

On their trips out to India, the Directors spent much time with us, either when they discussed Company matters with me, or when they returned to rest between their visits to the estates. They felt free to ask Susie whatever they wanted, and she was completely at ease with them. I guess it was perhaps the Chairman's idea that my wife should be given a trip to England in appreciation of all that she had done for every one of them.

After marriage, my daughter, Lulu, settled in Madras, a night's journey by train to The Nilgiris where I live. She pays me surprise visits now and again to see if I am all right, and to check if anything needs to be done about the house. On one such visit, she stayed longer than usual and undertook to clean out my study which also houses my library. By then, I had started writing this book with her constant urging not to give up, which would have been the easiest thing to do. While I was busy scribbling away, she came and handed me an old file without comment. I was dumbfounded to see in my wife's neat handwriting the complete menu for each meal that every Director had been served in our home from the time she married me. Susie's comments on the Director's reaction to the food appeared at the bottom of every page. It meant scrupulous attention to detail as each man had his particular likes and dislikes. As my wife had been entertaining all of them over the years, she knew everyone's preferences. When the Directors visited the Company's estates, I would prepare a comprehensive programme, and give Susie a copy so that she would know the days when they would stay with us, and especially the meals they would share at our table. Little did I know that each Director's visit to our home was planned so meticulously. Apart from her other qualifications, Susie was also an excellent cook. She would cook the dessert for each meal herself on a small kerosene stove that she kept in her storeroom.

Towards the end of January 1973, the Chairman wrote that the Board had approved in principle the idea of my wife accompanying me to England. We were to get there in June and stay for a month. Earlier, Col Williams had asked me to check out reasonably-priced flights, among other things, and I had provided all the information that I was able to gather in India from various sources. The Chairman said we were to travel as economically as possible, and also mentioned a sum of money that the Board had in mind to help meet our expenses in England. Although the amount of money indicated would not have covered our expenses in any way, it was a gesture that we appreciated. He added further, "We will all hope that it will be possible for you to bring Susie to our respective homes."

As it seemed almost definite that my wife and I would both go to England that year, I asked a dear friend, Roy Tharian (who is, sadly, not with us any more), if he could possibly arrange with one of his relations in the United States of America to remit foreign exchange on my behalf to Horrocks in the United Kingdom, the equivalent of which I would repay in rupees to whoever he nominated in India. To the eternal credit of Roy and his relation in America, the money was in London when I got there, and Horrocks handed it over to me.

Everything seemed to be straightforward, but the question of cheap flights came up again. For some time afterwards, my Chairman and I corresponded over low air fares. There were no cheap flights in India. I was asked to find out whether the amount spent on tickets bought in England, would be accepted as an expense. I forwarded the favourable view of the Company's auditors. I was beginning to get a little tired of the protracted correspondence on this subject which didn't seem to be too complicated when it was first raised. I lost interest and even didn't want to go England.

A cable arrived from the Board at the end of May 1973. There was some difficulty in arranging chartered flights, but the Board was still hopeful about sending out tickets for both of us around July. Meanwhile, as originally scheduled and approved by the Board, I went on long leave at the beginning of June, and provided the Board with details about where I could be contacted when I was away.

Early in June, soon after I left, another cable arrived for me in Peermade. The Board regretted, it said, that owing to the existing situation only I was invited to England that year, and that I should book an economy-class passage for myself alone in India. I was staying in Nagercoil then. As soon as I received the cable, I wrote immediately to the Company's travel agents in Cochin instructing them to book an economy-class return ticket for me. The Chairman wrote to me subsequently, incorporating the cable they had sent to Peermade, and explained that on the grounds of economy the Board could not bring my wife over, and that they were all very sorry to have taken that decision. After the hullabaloo of the past several months, I was astonished at the Board's decision. But I accepted it, and my wife took it very well, in spite of the fact that it was only because of the Board's invitation that she had applied for a passport and had obtained one after some difficulty.

By this time, I was with my mother in Padappai, a small village that is about an hour's drive from Madras. About the third week of June, the Head Office in Peermade received a cable from the Board to say that they were hoping to book me on Egypt Air, and that I should leave for London early in July. At the end of the month, when I was still in my village, I got the news that I had indeed been booked to fly by Egypt Air, and that the ticket was being sent out. Time was getting short, and it was confusion worst confounded. I wrote hurriedly to the travel agents in Cochin cancelling the booking I had made with them. It was all a case of trying to save a few rupees on the cost of one ticket. And, to make matters even more suspenseful, the ticket or rather the prepaid ticket voucher, arrived by ordinary post just the day before I had to leave the village to take my daughter back to her boarding school at the end of her school holidays.

It was the Board that had wanted me to go for official consultations to England, and it was the same Board that proposed I take my wife with me. The muddle they created was totally unnecessary, and the Directors didn't show the slightest remorse for meting out this treatment to me. As a matter of principle, if after careful consideration something is initiated, it must be successfully implemented. Just a few years earlier, when the Executives in the Company were mostly European, they went back and forth with their families as they were entitled to regular passages. No one talked about economizing on travel then. It was only when *I* had to go to England, as desired by the Board, that the cheapest form of travel was contemplated.

At some point when my travel plans were afoot, the Board had discovered that there were places in London called 'bucket shops' where airlines, especially some Middle Eastern ones, sold tickets at big discounts to attract customers. Egypt Air was obviously one of them. The object was to fill the aircraft to make a profit. The catch was that there was no guarantee that you would get a confirmed seat on the flight for which you were booked. This I was to discover later.

Soon after I took charge of the Company, I received a letter from Madden congratulating me and saying he wouldn't write much as "the Chairman liked all letters on Company matters to go through him and rightly so." About the same time that I received the cable from the Board early in June to say that they were withdrawing my wife's invitation, Madden wrote to me privately, part of which I must quote: "I am indeed sorry that we cannot bring both you and Susie to England this time; I am sure she will be bitterly disappointed and I have asked Col. Williams to emphasize our regret. I am afraid it is to be a working visit again instead of the holiday you had hoped for."

Madden was wrong. I had not hoped for a holiday in England. It was the Chairman who had written several months earlier to say that the Board had approved of our visit to England in June. Madden was now talking about emphasizing their regret. How was that going to help? I was reminded of the story of some small children who were going to school for the first time. Whenever the need arose, they would get up and toddle off to the toilet. The teacher thought she'd teach them some discipline. She said to them that whenever anyone wanted to go to the toilet to answer the first call of nature, he or she should put up one finger. One precocious little fellow gave the suggestion a moment's thought and came up with the classic comment, "How will that help, Miss?" Indeed.

Madden himself came and went in style. Unlike the other Directors who were on several Boards, Madden was a Director of only our Company with its three estates which he visited in leisurely fashion, taking several breaks in between. On his last visit, Madden stayed with us for ten nights off and on, and treated our house as his home away from home. While in

Peermade, he also visited the three estates in the district which were controlled by his Indian friend, the man who had advised him when I first joined SITE to deny me a living wage.

Madden was fond of saying that an Englishman's word is his bond. There is no such thing. Nobody can arrogate to himself any superior human virtue on the strength of his nationality. It is an individual thing, and a man's country of birth or the colour of his skin has nothing to do with it.

Travelling by Egypt Air was quite an experience. I don't know why I thought of it, but a day before I was due in Bombay to fly out to London, I asked one of my friends who was in Bombay on business to get my booking confirmed at the Egypt Air office. He agreed and gave me his telephone number in Bombay, saying that I should contact him as soon as I got there. When I arrived in Bombay, I spoke to my friend. He said that the reservation desk at Egypt Air had informed him that until the plane landed in Bombay they couldn't be too sure if a seat would be available or not. My friend had impressed upon them that I had to take that particular flight because I had an important Board meeting to attend soon after reaching London. They promised to help.

I walked over to the Egypt Air counter at the airport sometime before the plane bound for London was due to land. The counter was closed. Some young white people, backpackers, were hanging around. About half an hour before the plane landed, a prosperous-looking Egyptian came waving a ticket in front of him. He asked which one of us was Davidar. When I identified myself, he gave me a proper ticket and boarding pass in exchange for my ticket voucher and departed. The backpackers also left. They obviously knew the procedure from experience. My friend had done his bit and I was grateful.

On board the plane, I had to go looking for a vacant seat to occupy as the boarding pass did not indicate any in the normal manner. It was the same on every Egypt Air flight I took, both to and from London, or when I had to change planes in Cairo.

When I returned from London, I had to spend a whole day and night in Cairo before catching a plane to Bombay. The airline put up its passengers in a new five-star hotel which was situated fairly close to the famous pyramids, listed as one of the Seven Wonders of the World. I went up the Great Pyramid of Cheops, named after an Egyptian Pharaoh of the same name, which it is said took twenty years to build. The visit was an awesome experience.

After dinner that night in Cairo, I walked out onto the road just outside the hotel gate. There were some ramshackle taxis and a few professional guides hanging about. I told one guide I wanted to see some authentic belly dancing. He told me that he would take me to King Farouk's favourite nightclub. Farouk had been dead some eight years by then, but he had a reputation of being a connoisseur of female flesh. So, off we went. In the nightclub, there was an open-air stage, around which we sat on chairs at a lower level. I was shown a large room at the back with a wide window. Apparently, Farouk sat there with his companions and watched the show in front of him without being seen himself. Unfortunately, it was the belly dancer's night off. In her place, another dancer did some form of Oriental dance and gyrated furiously to some frenetic music before becoming briefly topless as she glided into the green room. She was probably some Continental dancer, and I was sorry I missed what I had come out to see.

I suppose I may not have had an opportunity to see the Pyramids if I didn't have to take a cheap flight by Egypt Air. But it was poor compensation for the anxious moments I had to endure. Moreover, it was not a dignified way to travel, and no senior Executive of a Company, of any Company, should be subjected to such a horrible experience when he has to fly on Company business.

Being the only man who seemed concerned, Col Williams asked me if it was okay flying by Egypt Air while we were waiting to have lunch at a restaurant after the first Board meeting. Before I could reply, one Director intervened and said they had saved much money because I had travelled by that airline. The Chairman fell silent. After lunch, we returned to the boardroom, from where everyone left for their homes except John in whose house I was to spend the night. He mumbled something and left the room. I stood around for some time, and when he did not reappear, I went looking for him. There was a long corridor separating the two wings on that floor. By a strange coincidence or perhaps it was pre-planned, the wing on either side of the corridor had two firms of Secretaries, Rowe, White & Co (mine), and M P Evans & Co. Both served identical interests, namely, plantations in the East. I found John in a large room belonging to the M P Evans side of the corridor, standing near a very tall man. It occurred to me afterwards that they were waiting for me. John introduced me to the man, again mumbling his name which I didn't catch. John was a great mumbler.

I didn't know what it was all about. Things were going to be different in the near future, yet no one let me in on what they might be. When we were alone, Col Williams vaguely mentioned that he had told John that regular correspondence with India, as was now taking place, was essential but that John didn't think it was necessary. More riddles.

Anyway, the tall man followed us to John's house where we all had tea. After tea, there was some conversation about our Company. As night fell, the three of us drove to a hotel for dinner, many miles away. At dinner and afterwards, John and the tall man were engaged in earnest conversation, nothing of which made any sense to me. But I was not listening anyhow. And, John didn't tell me what was going on either.

When the business for which I was called was completed, I returned to India. I was still none the wiser. A few months later, I received news that the tall man I had met in England was visiting the Company's estates. When he arrived and started talking, things slowly started falling into place. There were going to be changes, and far-reaching ones at that, in the administrative set-up of the Company. I wasn't aware if Col Williams was still the Chairman, but he certainly didn't write the usual weekly letters as before. A merger of the two firms of Secretaries was on the cards, and as Col Williams was due to retire, the firm M P Evans & Co would also administer the erstwhile estates of Rowe, White & Co. John wrote a letter to the effect that regular letters might be discontinued in the "present circumstances" (what circumstances?), and that if I had to write about some important matter, "it would be helpful if the first page of the letter was endorsed with 'urgent reply wanted' or 'cabled reply wanted'."

At dinner the first night he spent with us, the tall man told my wife and me that he was basically a 'rubber man', and that John might become the Chairman of SITE. John had been a Director of the Company long enough to know what was going on, despite being an accountant, not a planter. On his first visit when I was acting for the General Manager and staying in the General Manager's bungalow several years earlier, John was initially suspicious about all things Indian, me included, but later he became more human and felt he could trust me. I knew I could get on with John almost as well as I got on with Col Williams. That was not the first time that the tall man was to say something, and then change his mind and say something totally different on the same subject afterwards.

The next day, I took the tall man down to my office. He had done his homework albeit selectively. As soon as he entered my private room, and even before he sat down, he said to me, "Look, why do you want to transfer the Superintendents, it'll upset them." I was taken aback. The man hadn't met any of the other Executives in the Company, nor had he visited any of the estates. I was surprised that he could make a statement of that nature. Fortunately, it was not my idea.

A year earlier, when I attended my first Board meeting in London, I was given a copy of the agenda listing the various matters that would be discussed. 'Rotation of Estate Charges' was one of them. The Directors were unanimously of the opinion that "management charges should be changed at not less than three years nor more than five." And, I was to carry out the transfers. I don't know why the Directors thought of it, but the decision was welcome. Things were beginning to go wrong, and the Board had felt that as a matter of policy the periodic transfer of Superintendents would be beneficial to the Company. It was the accepted custom in the Company to finally post men with long years of service either to an estate where they could live and work until they retired, or to promote them to the post of General Manager. None of the Superintendents who worked under me at that time were senior enough to be given charge of an estate on a permanent basis.

The two acting Superintendents subsequently became regular Superintendents, and they were about to complete five years on their respective estates in a few months' time. A senior Superintendent had been recruited by the Company four years earlier. The tall man must have had access to the minutes of the Board meetings that had been held in 1972 and 1973, and he wanted to challenge the decision of the Board with me in India. When I patiently explained, in some detail, the circumstances which had prompted the Board's decision he said he agreed with them.

As the tall man was completely new to the Company's estates, I thought I would generally put him in the picture, and tell him something about the performance of each estate. I kept a comparative chart which showed, at a glance, all the relevant details pertaining to each estate, month by month. I showed it to him thinking he might be interested. The man was brusque. He said to me, in not too friendly a manner, that I was not to tell him anything, and that he would go round the estates and form his own opinion about everything. I shut up and mentally wished him the very best of luck when he set out on his visits to the estates.

When he returned, he was breathing fire. On his own accord, he asked me to show him my chart. Our first meeting on the ground didn't strike me as having exactly got off to an auspicious start.

∼

The Old Order Changeth

"The old order changeth, yielding place to the new.........," said the poet Alfred, Lord Tennyson. I was soon to experience first-hand what he meant. I learnt who the members of the new Board of Directors of my Company were, and John was not the Chairman. The tall man – the No.1 of the firm of Secretaries which had merged with my old one – had made himself Chairman.

In March 1974, four months after the tall man, who was later to become the Chairman, paid his first visit to the estates, I received a letter from John. He indicated that I should continue with the management of two estates consequent upon Glenmary Estate being sold. This was news to me even though the new Chairman had mentioned to me that in view of the losses incurred by Glenmary which resulted in the poor performance of the Company, something drastic needed to be done. I was told that planning for the future should be confined to the other two estates, Ladrum and Kuduakarnam.

As the Board asked me to make discreet enquiries about the possible sale of Glenmary Estate, I broached the subject with our Tea Brokers. I was told while it was not immediately possible, perhaps later when trading conditions improved as they were likely to do in the not too distant future, the estate could be sold at favourable terms.

In the two years that followed, I was privy to a series of events that disillusioned me considerably. The details will be of no interest to the general reader, so I will merely say that it was dispiriting to see the Company for which I had worked so hard being offered to buyers, some of whom seemed quite unsuitable from my point of view. Many of the Company's systems and procedures were jettisoned, and the uncertainty of the Company's fate made matters worse.

In the past, at the beginning of each week without fail, a letter arrived from the Secretaries, signed by the Chairman himself. It was known as the 'London letter' because it originated from there. I would reply two or three days later, providing explanations that were sought or asking for something or the other to be sanctioned. This system had been in existence for quite some time, certainly from the time that I joined the Company. Under the new dispensation, the 'London letter' was in limbo much of the time. I would wait and wait for some decision to be taken, and then a long cable would arrive, followed by a longer letter. It was all very unsettling. I couldn't see what purpose, if any, would be served by my hanging around, notwithstanding the good job I had with nobody in sight to supplant me. In fact, when John first introduced me to the Chairman-to-be he said, "There is a serious problem of succession." The tall man turned to me and asked if I was leaving. When I replied in the negative, he said, "Ah, well, we don't have a problem now, do we?" So, one evening after tea, I told my wife, Susie, that we should go for a walk as I wished to discuss something important with her.

When I first joined the Company, my Superintendent, Richardson, wanted me to be present when he made the weekly payments to the labour on the estate every Friday afternoon. The end of the payments signalled the close of the day's work, and Richardson would then invite me to take tea with him and his wife. At that time, he was staying in the General Manager's bungalow, a short distance from the estate office, as his bungalow on Woodlands was being set right. Richardson never gossiped, but one day as we were having tea, he told me that walls have ears, indirectly warning me to be careful about what I said inside the house. I remembered his advice.

Eddy Davidar,
Ranikoil Bungalow,
circa 1956

Ranikoil Division, Ladrum Estate, 1958

(L to R) Philip Davis, Andrew Boyd Spence, Eddy Davidar, Dennis Boas, Henry Allan Boas, the Peermade Club bar, 4 November 1956

Eddy Davidar, Trafalgar Square, London, July 1957

Eddy Davidar
weds
Sushila Kamalam,
St George's Cathedral, Madras,
8 January 1958

Mrs Helen Madden (partly hidden) assists the newly-weds as they cut their
wedding cake, St George's Cathedral grounds, Madras, 8 January 1958

Susie and Eddy Davidar, Ladrum Estate, circa 1964

*Jai and Lulu,
Ladrum Estate,
circa 1963*

Eddy Davidar and CJ Madden, Ladrum Estate, 1965

Ladrum Bungalow, circa 1965

Asha looks out of the Hudson car, Ladrum Estate, 1959

Susie Davidar with the jungle sheep Bambi, Ladrum Estate, 1963

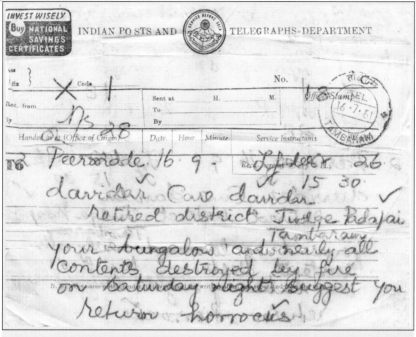

INVEST WISELY Buy NATIONAL SAVINGS CERTIFICATES

INDIAN POSTS AND TELEGRAPHS DEPARTMENT

The telegram announcing the Glenmary Bungalow fire, July 1961

The gutted Glenmary Bungalow, July 1961

Christopher Calver,
circa 1955

(L to R) Heather Lovatt, Susie Davidar, Mrs Henry Longhurst, Denise Lovatt, circa 1961

(L to R) Lorraine Nicholl,
Susie Davidar with Jai,
Alex York with Mark Nicholl,
Chris Nicholl (standing
behind Lorraine), circa 1960

Oswald William Horrocks
in retirement in England,
13 September 1969

Eddy Davidar in retirement with Flossie,
Wellington, The Nilgiris, 26 June 2005

While we walked, not a soul was in sight. I told Susie that I was finding it difficult to carry on with my job because of the suspense that was becoming unbearable at times – mental stress can be devastating. I asked her what her reaction would be if I quit. My wife could have put up valid objections to the idea. Both our children were still studying – our son was at university and our daughter was in high school. And at my age, I wouldn't have got another job even if I wanted one. But with a woman's intuition, she must have known what was going on. All she said was, "Any time you say." I felt happy that if I had to take the ultimate step, there would at least be no unhappiness on the home front.

☙

Finis

The year was 1975. I pondered the fateful decision of finally packing it in, and it took me quite a while to make up my mind. The Government of India brought into force the Foreign Exchange Regulation Act (FERA), 1973, which stipulated that all fully-owned foreign Companies, of which mine was one being a sterling Company, had to dilute their shareholding by forming a local (rupee) Company in which Indian shareholders were to be offered a minimum of twenty six per cent of the capital, while the foreign Company could retain seventy four per cent. This new development gave me a lot of work to do, work that none of my predecessors had to cope with, and I was to sail in uncharted waters.

I received a letter from John early in November to say that the Chairman would be in Sri Lanka (formerly Ceylon) for two days in the third week of November. He said in view of the latest Government order, it would be helpful if I could meet him there to have a discussion. It was not easy to go to Sri Lanka at such short notice. I had to get a separate visa from their country's representative in Madras, which I managed with some local influence. The Reserve Bank of India sanctioned me the grand sum of five pounds, and I promptly lost the one five pound note that I was given even before I took off from Madras.

I met the Chairman in Sri Lanka, and told him about matters that had to be tackled on an urgent basis. He said to me that on my return to India I should ask the Company's lawyers to set in motion the initial steps to form a local Company on the basis of seventy four per cent shares to be owned by the present

SITE Company, placing the remaining twenty six per cent with locally-known interested parties. After he returned to England, he wrote to me confidentially, asking me to enquire if forty per cent of the capital of the new Indian Company was taken up by Indian shareholders, could the sale proceeds of that forty per cent be remitted to the United Kingdom. If it was not possible, then seventy four per cent would be owned by the SITE Company, and twenty six per cent by local shareholders. I was also instructed to investigate the possibility of a complete sale of the assets of SITE in India, if the remittance from the sale of the forty per cent shareholding was not allowed to the United Kingdom.

He went on to say that if a local Company was formed, I would be the Managing Director, and also the Chairman's alternate in India. John would be the other UK representative. The other Directors on the Board would depend on Indian participation. By now it was clear that the new regulations had accelerated the Board's decision to sell the Company in whole or in part. It was no longer a question of if but when.

At the end of February 1976, I received a letter from John saying that the events in Sri Lanka made it necessary for him to visit that country, and he proposed to meet me on his return trip. The sole purpose of his visit was to have discussions with people who might be interested in taking up shares in the new rupee Company when it was formed. Along with his letter, he sent me the complete itinerary of his visit to India, from 3 March when he would arrive in Trivandrum in Kerala, until he left the country from Bombay on 12 March. He also said that he had made his own travel arrangements. It seemed obvious that someone who knew South India well had helped to draw up his itinerary, for I was pretty sure that John didn't know some of the places where he was going to stay during his trip – two nights at the Ooty Club in The Nilgiris for example. He asked me to accompany him, and wanted me to be present when he met with various people, including an Agency in the textile industry in Bombay. He felt it would be useful if I was at the meeting with this firm, in case they decided to take a financial stake in the new Company. I was intrigued how he found out about these people in Bombay, whom I gathered were connected in some way with the Tata empire.

After talks with the representatives of several firms during the week following his arrival, John and I eventually wound up at the Coimbatore airport, from where we were to drive up to Ooty for meetings in The Nilgiris, the final stage of his sojourn. When our business engagements in The Nilgiris were done, we had to get to Bangalore by road, so that we could take a flight to Bombay, from where John would fly out to the United Kingdom. John had not been to The Nilgiris at any time previously, and he watched with fascination the scenery that unfolded before him. The hillsides were a lot less crowded thirty years ago. John was impressed with all he saw. We drove through Wellington, and a few miles farther on, John said to me, "Eddy, when you eventually retire, you should come and live somewhere here." He couldn't have been more prophetic, as we came to live in The Nilgiris, in Wellington, to be precise, in about a year from then.

From Ooty, we drove to Coonoor the next day, so that John could meet the No.1 of a firm of Managing Agents in Coonoor, an Englishman who had been angling for our Company for some time. The discussions were over at the end of the afternoon, and the Englishman offered to drop us himself at the Ooty Club. On the way, he told John about his firm and his boss. He said his boss was a better type of Marwari (he pronounced the word 'Mahwahree'). After a few visits to India, John could just about recognize an Indian, and to be told there were different kinds of Indians, and that in the same community there were good and bad Indians, was, I thought, far too much for him to take in. When he didn't quite understand something, John would say 'Hmmm' and leave it at that. This was one such

situation. There was another amusing incident on our trip when
he said 'Hmmm' all the time, but we shall hear about it later.

On our way to Ooty, we had to cross an iron bridge,
popularly known as the Black Bridge, which connects the main
road leading to Ooty with the Wellington Cantonment. Black
Bridge also marks the limits of the military area on one side.
There is a bus stop on the other side of the bridge, and a bus
from Ooty was standing there, correctly parked on the left-
hand side of the road. The Englishman had to veer a little to
the left to get to the middle of the main road at this point, well
away from where the bus was standing, before proceeding
uphill. The man was obviously used to driving on the wrong
side of the road at this intersection, so he was annoyed that
the bus was in the way. He got as close to the bus as possible,
stopped near the driver and shouted at him for being in the
way, then drove on imperiously.

John saw all this happen. That night after dinner, while we
were sitting around chatting, he said to me, "Surely, the bus
driver in Wellington was in the right, wasn't he? Why did this
fellow shout at him?" I told him quietly that in India some
white people like this boorish Englishman could still behave
the way he did and get away with it, thirty years after the
country had become independent. John was a good friend and
I could be frank with him. He was a sensitive man, and all he
could do was to shake his head.

On another occasion in Coonoor, I saw a white man,
someone I knew, park his car where apparently he shouldn't
have. A policeman standing a little distance away blew on his
whistle and signalled him to get moving. The man smiled at
me and told the cop to go to hell. He then left the car where
he'd parked it, and walked away. The policeman did nothing,
and resumed talking to a buddy who was with him. Two
centuries of being made to feel inferior does take its toll.

Almost ten years after I had retired, I had one last letter
from John, who kept in touch off and on. He said that he had

retired from his executive duties the previous year, even though he continued to serve on the Boards of many Companies. He had travelled to various parts of the world including Australia and America in the course of business, and said he felt that Wellington in The Nilgiris was a lovely part of the world. I couldn't agree with him more. He also added that he often thought back to the old days – before they sold out to the 'Mahwahree' – and of the wonderful drive round South India that we undertook together.

From Ooty, we had to drive through Mysore to get to Bangalore. Whoever had prepared John's itinerary in England had told him that he must not fail to visit the fabulous palace of the Maharaja of Mysore. John asked me if we could do so.

As we reached Mysore, I told the driver to take us to the palace. When we got there, we found the iron gate at the entrance locked. We could see some policemen lounging about quite close to the gate. Through the bars, I beckoned to the non-commissioned officer (NCO) in charge, and he came over and stood on the other side of the gate. I asked him if we could go inside to look around. I spoke in Tamil which the man could understand. He told me that a film was being shot inside the palace, so nobody could gain entry. I pleaded with him, and, pointing to John, said that this Englishman had come all the way from England to see the palace, and would be most disappointed indeed if he was turned away. The man wavered a bit. I took out a currency note from my wallet and held it before him, a tip in advance if you like. He took the note and asked us to return at one o'clock in the afternoon. We had plenty of time to catch the plane at Bangalore that evening for Bombay, so we had lunch at a hotel that served Western food, and came back promptly at the time indicated.

The NCO spotted us and came and opened the gate. He was sorry that we could not be shown around the palace because of the orders he had received, but he offered to take us on a guided tour of the extensive palace grounds. For John's benefit, he spoke in his own brand of English and while I could understand some of it, I knew that John was not with us. He kept saying, though, every now and then, almost automatically, 'Hmmm', to encourage the man. Dotted about the lawn were some small cannons, pieces of artillery from the days of yore, which fired a single ball, inflicting whatever damage they could on the enemy positions. Every time we passed one of these cannons, the NCO would pat it lovingly and say 'braash'. John would nod his head and say 'Hmmm'. After the third cannon, the policeman became suspicious of John's reaction and said to me, "Vaat, 'e no unnersan ingleesh?" Predictably, John said 'Hmmm'. I laughed. John wanted to know what I was laughing at. When I told him, he guffawed. Anyway, our little tour came to an end. I thanked the policeman for his kindness, and gave him another currency note, the balance tip. He was most grateful and saluted us when we left.

John departed for England early on 13 March. Ten days later, I received a personal letter from him, thanking me for my help on his visit to India. He also said that the trip was 'highly successful', and promised to keep me briefed on further developments. That was the last I heard from him, as the Chairman himself took over all the subsequent correspondence. It soon became apparent that the Chairman was the only one to take all the decisions of the Board, and John was completely sidelined.

Two months after I received John's letter, the Chairman wrote to me, saying in effect that if the scheme they were considering came to fruition, whereby an outside buyer (the Marwari, whose man we'd met in Coonoor) would invest in the Company, then my own position would become precarious. In other words, I would have to go. Just a few months earlier, the man had told me, in writing, not once but twice, that I would become the Managing Director of the new Indian Company when it was formed. The man did not even bother to apologize for reneging on the offer he had made to me not so long ago. Strangely, the thought of losing a good job through no fault of mine did not affect me one bit. The feeling was actually one of relief, as my own efforts to leave in the past had not borne fruit. There was now some hope that I might be able to get out of tea planting in the not too distant future after all.

The Chairman had been very busy dictating letters to various people on the same day he served me notice to quit. I gathered this information from the copies of the letters he sent to keep me informed, all of which had the same date. They were long letters as usual, and were addressed to our Company lawyers in Kottayam, our auditors in Madras, and the head of the Agency House in Coonoor which was largely owned by the Marwari businessman. The letter he wrote to me was the shortest of all.

A couple of weeks after our lawyers and I received word that a final decision had been taken about who would buy the Company, I received a phone call from a senior member of a prominent proprietary planting family in Mundakayam, which was situated a few miles down the hill from Peermade, towards Kottayam. He was the eldest of three brothers resident in Mundakayam, all mostly rubber planters. I knew the two younger brothers somewhat, but I didn't know the oldest brother at all. I had seen him occasionally before, but he generally kept aloof and seemed a distant figure. Naturally, therefore, I was intrigued by his call.

This brother said that he wanted to talk to me about an important matter, but he did not want to come up to my bungalow as he wanted the meeting to be kept a secret. If I was willing, he proposed that we meet that evening in a friend's house that was hardly used by the owner. He explained in detail how to get to the house which was a few miles away from my estate and towards Mundakayam. Though rather close to the main road, it was tucked away inside. This was all cloak-and-dagger stuff.

By the time I arrived, my host was already there. There was no electricity, so he had got the caretaker of the house to light a petromax lantern. He had brought along a bottle of whisky, Johnnie Walker, Black Label – an honour. Scotch whisky was a rare commodity at that time, and was not readily available in the open market.

We settled down to chat on the verandah, seated comfortably and with our glasses charged. The gentleman told me that some people known to him were interested in taking over our Company on the basis of transfer of shares. He said that the negotiated sum of money would be paid in pounds sterling over a period of two years or so. He knew our lawyers, especially the senior partner intimately whom he had approached with this proposal, but was told that it might be a little too late. Consequently, he had decided to meet me and ask if I would convey to my Board his friends' interest in my Company. I promised to do so. I heard later from one of the Directors, not John, that the Chairman had received my letter outlining the terms of this new offer, and had decided that if the current scheme did not fructify for some reason or the other, this alternative would be considered.

With the business for which he had come up out of the way, the gentleman started talking about other things. He did tell me, though, that if they succeeded in getting hold of my Company, they would kick out all the other fellows but retain me to train the boys who would be brought in. And then, he told me a story. Many years earlier, his father had gone to see JS Wilkie, the General Manager of the Company, about some matter that concerned them both. Wilkie was known for his autocratic ways, and had not invited this man's father into the bungalow but had talked to him in the garden and had sent him away. That had hurt. This eminent planter went on to say that here he was enjoying the privilege of having a drink with the General Manager of the same Company many years later. I nearly fell out of my chair. He had always struck me as a strong silent type, and to think that *he* felt honoured to entertain *me* took some digesting.

In the months that followed, I was to witness the Chairman's insensitive handling of Company matters. While I waited impatiently to know when I would be able to leave, there was a development that worked in my favour, and I was able to write to my Chairman and tell him that I would like to leave by 1 March 1977 when the Company's new financial year would begin, if not earlier. His reply accepting my resignation took a long time in coming. When it eventually did, he had accepted my proposed date of departure. His letter arrived two days before Christmas 1976. I took it home and gave it to my wife, Susie, with the comment, "Our Christmas present." She read the letter without showing the slightest emotion and handed it back to me. There used to be a British Chancellor of the Exchequer in the 1950s by the name of Lord RA 'RAB' Butler. I believe he was famous for saying, "Don't be elated, never be depressed," which Horrocks quoted often. Susie was like him.

After the question of my retirement was settled, I wrote one last letter to my Chairman early in January 1977. I mentioned that I anticipated that the fortunes of the Company were due to show a great upward leap. I wrote, "It is a matter of much comfort and consolation that I am able to leave the Company at a time when production and profits will have reached levels that have been never attained before." I had the satisfaction of knowing that my expectations were more than fully realized.

At about the same time, I wrote to the auditor in Madras who visited the estates every year to carry out the annual audit of the Company's accounts, seeking his advice on some tax matters. The man was a junior partner, and though he belonged to a different caste than all the other partners in the firm, they kept him on as he was their tax expert, and they needed his expertise. In my letter I also mentioned that we hoped to make a large profit that year, on account of the bountiful crops that we had harvested and the remunerative prices that we had been receiving. He replied saying that he was also of the opinion that the Company would make the highest profit that it ever had in any year, and agreed that I couldn't leave the services of the Company at a better time. I had earlier advised him to read the book, *The Power of Positive Thinking* by Norman Vincent Peale which I believed would help him overcome his passive acceptance of the bullying tactics of a senior partner in his firm. He thanked me in his letter for my suggestion, and on a subsequent visit, he told me that when the senior partner came one day to bully him, he stood up to him which took the other man completely by surprise. The senior partner started retreating to his own room, but my friend chased after him and told him that he was not finished yet, and attacked him some more. My friend said to me that after that one occasion, he was left totally in peace. I would advise anybody who is ever assailed by self-doubt to read this book. I have known of at least two other people who have benefited enormously from reading it.

As I was handing over charge to the representative of the newly-appointed Managing Agents, I received a letter from their No.1 in Coonoor to say, "Certainly you are handing over at a time of record crops and earnings and we much appreciate the cooperation." It was good of him to say so, given his earlier superior attitude.

It was perhaps my friend John who put things in the proper perspective. On the eve of my departure from Peermade, he finally broke his silence, almost a year since I last heard from him. He wrote me a letter in which he said, "You joined S.I.T.E. within a year that I joined Rowe, White & Co and it seems a very long time ago. During most of the period that you have been General Manager, the whole tea industry has suffered dreadful economic problems and it has always been a great comfort to know that your capable and steady hands were at the helm during that time and all of your friends here, both past and present Directors, wish you and Suzy every happiness in your well-earned retirement." Blowing my own trumpet? Perhaps. To quote Horrocks once again, "If you don't blow your own trumpet, nobody'll blow it for you."

As soon as I announced to the Executive Staff that the Company would change hands imminently, my wife and I and our daughter took off to The Nilgiris in search of a house to buy. Of all the houses that we saw, my daughter, Lulu, liked the one we saw in Wellington the best. We have never regretted for one moment our decision to buy Flo-Iris, despite the problems we've had from time to time. I still live in it, happily.

On 1 March 1977, as we went down the hill for the last time, I felt a great load slipping from my shoulders. You read about this kind of experience in books, but I actually felt it, physically. Free at last. I had wanted to leave Peermade on several occasions before, but the opportunity never presented itself. William Shakespeare put the words in the mouth of Hamlet, Prince of Denmark, in his famous play *Hamlet* when he said, "There is a divinity that shapes our ends, Rough-hew them how we will." I believe the bard was right.

∾

PART TWO

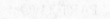

Adventures in Shikar

O ne of the main reasons why I chose to become a planter was the opportunities for shikar that such a life offered apart from being able to work in the outdoors. I come from a family of *shikaris* who have now all become ardent conservationists. Among us, the best known in the sport is my older brother, Reggie, who has shot a tiger (every *shikari's* ambition) and a rogue elephant (an unusual achievement); and, after becoming a conservationist, turned to 'shoot' them with his camera equally successfully.

All of us started with an airgun the moment we were big enough to hold one. Our first airgun was a .177 bore Tell (presumably named after William Tell, the legendary Swiss hero who split an apple on his son's head with his bow and arrow); we then graduated to a slightly heavier .22 bore before finally getting to handle a shotgun. Every year, the courts were closed in the summer for two months during which time my father would take us out on shikar trips. When we didn't go shooting waterbirds in the lakes a few miles outside Trichinopoly, my father would take us to a small town called Perambalur, about thirty miles or so away from Trichinopoly, where we would camp for a few days. Panthers, bears and wild boar could be shot in the jungle there, even though we never got any. Interestingly, many of our workers on the Ranikoil division of Ladrum Estate came from Perambalur, so I discovered when I worked there.

When I joined the Army, I did not possess a weapon of my own. I had the use of a Service rifle which belonged to a *jawan* who was always with me when we went out on field exercise, and I zeroed it to my way of taking aim. I used it most effectively whenever we went out on shikar, which was quite frequently, when my regiment was posted to peace stations during the first two years of my Army career.

When I became a planter, I still did not own a firearm. I had to content myself with going out in the evenings after work to look for wildlife. My first experience was seeing a pair of muntjac or barking deer, so named because their call when heard from afar, and more so when they are alarmed, resembles a dog barking. Barking deer are commonly known though as jungle sheep. One evening, soon after I joined Glenmary Estate, I walked up the hill behind my bungalow after tea and sat down beside the well from which my bungalow was supplied with water by gravity. Except for a sparsely-wooded *shola* of red gum trees, which would be used in the factory tea dryers some day, there was tea all around. The *shola* was about a hundred yards from where I was sitting, straight across from me, and there was a large open space in the middle of it. A movement in the open space caught my attention, and it turned out to be a pair of jungle sheep gambolling about. From then on, and until the South-West monsoon broke about two months later, I went every evening to my well and sat down and watched the jungle sheep playing around. It was all very peaceful as no other human being came up there. Jungle sheep are very predictable in their habits. They will appear at the same place and practically at the same time on most days. This habit of theirs costs them their lives, if anybody owned a gun on the estate and was keen on shikar. They are also curious animals, and will stop and stare at any object that distracts them, often spelling their doom.

A Tea Maker and a worker in the Company owned a shotgun each, and often they would go looking for game. They would shoot these animals if they knew where to find them as they were such easy targets. After about six years, I got back to Glenmary as a Superintendent having served in various other places in the Company. The first thing I did was to seek out my jungle sheep. But they were gone. I could only hope they had not been shot. But I am getting ahead of my story.

When I was close to completing one year in SITE, Madden, the General Manager, told me that since I was on basic pay and dearness allowance, at the end of one year of service, I would be given a bonus of one thousand rupees. That was great news. I could at last realize my ambition of owning a firearm of my own, and could also buy myself a radio set so that I could listen to music every night.

I decided to buy myself a 15-shot BSA .22 rifle with the bonus I was sanctioned. Seven years after the country became independent, it was still possible to acquire a firearm manufactured abroad from arms dealers in Bombay. All you had to do was to send them your arms licence and ask them to send the weapon of your choice by Value Payable by Post (VPP). I planned to acquire mine from The Bombay Armoury.

I applied for my rifle licence to the issuing authorities in Kottayam, our district headquarters, fifty miles away. Most of our supplies were obtained from there. The Company's lawyers also had their office in Kottayam. As I heard nothing about my licence for a considerable period of time, I wrote to the Company's lawyers and requested them to enquire about the fate of my application. They replied promptly to say that my application had been sent to the Police Station in Peermade sometime earlier for their verification, and that the police report was awaited.

Armed with this disclosure, I hopped onto my motorcycle and went to the Police Station. It was drizzling heavily, and it was also quite cold. At the Police Station, I found only the Station Writer and enquired if my application for a rifle licence had been received by them from Kottayam for their verification and report. He admitted cheerfully that it had, and that my information was correct. When I asked him why nothing had been done about it in all this time, he didn't reply me directly but drew my attention to the fact that it was a cold evening. I agreed that it was indeed a little nippy, but for the life of me, I couldn't understand how the evening being cold had anything to do with the police inaction over my application for so long. He went on to say that if something was imbibed, it would greatly help to alleviate the chill in his bones. I got the drift. Right across the road from the Police Station, down a long flight of steps, was a liquor shop. He was suggesting in an indirect way that if I helped to ward off the cold by making a contribution, it would be greatly appreciated. I gave him some money which I reckoned would buy a half bottle of rum, and asked him to get himself one. He thanked me profusely. Emboldened by his response, I asked him if the police verification would now be attended to. He assured me that he would speak to the Sub-Inspector the very next day, and that something would be done about it. I also added that he could inform the Sub-Inspector that if he, the Sub-Inspector, should care to come to my bungalow the following evening, there would be something for him also.

Spencer's, the store where I had a credit account, was almost next door to the Police Station, and it was still open. I went in and collected a bottle of Hayward's Piccadilly Gin before going home. Sure enough, the next evening, just as I finished having my tea, a car came to a halt outside my bungalow in a cloud of smoke. The Sub-Inspector had arrived. He had commandeered the only ramshackle taxi in town to come and see me.

I invited the man in, and told him that I had come to his Station the previous evening. He said that he had been so informed, and had also got my message. I picked up the bottle of gin and gave it to him. He accepted it gratefully. I offered him a cup of tea but he declined. Instead, he merely asked for a sheet of newspaper in which he carefully wrapped the bottle. Then, he took leave of me. I asked if the police report would now be dispatched. He assured me the matter would be taken care of immediately. The Sub-Inspector was as good as his word. Not too long afterwards, my licence arrived by post.

I sent off my licence to the dealer in Bombay, and asked for the rifle to be sent to me at the earliest by VPP. Within days, I heard that my rifle was on its way. I still remember that my rifle cost me about two hundred rupees, including packaging and postage, which was most reasonable.

As soon as my rifle arrived, I took it and went down to the red gum *shola* (it had a lot of scrub inside) at the bottom of my division, Ranikoil, to look for some game. Ironically, the first thing that I saw was a jungle sheep. It was not too far from where I was standing on the narrow footpath inside the *shola*. It was just above me, and was looking down curiously at me. I took careful aim and fired. Instead of falling down as I had expected the animal to do, it turned and raced up the hill through the scrub and disappeared. I was most dismayed to have missed a big target at close range. In the Army, I could pick off even moving targets at a distance with my Service rifle.

I mentioned this incident to John Lovatt in the Club one day. John worked for TTE, our sister sterling Company, and was a renowned *shikari*. He had shot his tiger, and was always talking about where he was going to hang its pelt in his *oodu* (house) in England. John interspersed his speech with a smattering of Tamil, and certainly knew more words than his compatriots in the district. And, he used them in the right context too. I happened to see the tiger pelt on a wall in his house in England many years later, and it was certainly in the right place. John told me that jungle sheep sometimes had the habit of running away after being wounded, and would drop dead some distance away. John knew his jungle lore.

I did not get a chance to shoot jungle sheep on the same division again, although I shot jungle fowl which were plentiful in the same *shola* for the pot. About two years later, I was transferred to the Woodlands division on Glenmary Estate. Just behind the bungalow which was quite far from the labour lines and staff quarters on this division, there was a red gum *shola*. You just had to pick up your rifle and walk into the *shola* to find game. Soon after I moved into the bungalow, I walked up the path in the *shola* with my rifle one day. I hadn't gone far when I saw a jungle sheep standing close at hand, looking at me. I took careful aim and fired. This animal, too, turned around and bounded off as though nothing had happened. I couldn't see the animal, but I could tell where it was headed by the scrub shaking along the path it was taking. I kept watching. About fifty yards or so from where it was shot at, I saw one bush in particular shaking for a couple of minutes before it went still. I followed the trail of the jungle sheep, and when I reached the bush that trembled, the animal was lying dead there. John Lovatt was right.

I was still looking at the jungle sheep, when a man appeared at my side. It was Michael, an attendant in the Company's Group Hospital which was situated on my division. Michael was in the habit of walking beyond the *shola* to collect the lush grass that grew there for his cows. Michael helped to carry the slain animal down to my bungalow, and stayed to collect his share of the meat and some for the doctor at Woodlands Hospital.

About three years later, I was back again on Ranikoil division, but this time around, I was a married man with a baby son. I had by now acquired John Lovatt's John Rigby .400/.350 sporting rifle as he had given up shooting. This weapon was a beauty and perfectly balanced. One evening after tea I took this rifle and went for a walk down the main road, not really expecting to see anything. A couple of hundred yards or so from the bungalow, there was some low scrub above the tea, and standing in it, in fading light, was a jungle sheep. It was the first time that I was going to use this sporting rifle which was vastly more powerful than my .22 rifle. I aimed at the animal and fired. It just dropped where it stood. A man who was coming up the road saw me shoot the animal. He went through the tea and brought it down, and carried it up to my bungalow. He placed it in front of the bungalow under a light. It looked so beautiful that I swore I would never again shoot a jungle sheep. I never did.

My life with jungle sheep was not quite over though.

I took charge of Ladrum Estate in November 1962 when Horrocks retired from planting after almost forty years with the same Company. I had been on the estate barely a few months when a worker turned up one day at lunchtime with a tiny jungle sheep kid (if that is what you call the young one of a jungle sheep). He said he and his fellow workers were weeding in a field nearby when they came across this little thing. Presumably, it was abandoned by its mother when she was disturbed by all the activity around her. The man asked if we would like to keep it. Of course, we would. My wife, Susie, gave the kid a little diluted milk in a feeding bottle. After some hesitation – it was probably afraid – the baby animal drank the milk quite avidly. Susie took complete charge of the little jungle sheep. She looked after its nourishment, and stayed with it much of the time. The jungle sheep grew rapidly. It may not have been terribly original a name, but we called our pet Bambi as she was a female. Bambi took to my wife, and followed her everywhere like Mary's little lamb in the nursery rhyme. We had a random-bred dog, Asha. She had fox terrier blood – her mother was one. She came to us as a wedding present five years earlier, and if ever a dog was a man's best friend, it was Asha. She was devoted to the family, and would religiously go for a walk every morning with our two children, Jai and Lulu. Asha also took to Bambi, and they became the best of friends.

There was a large lawn in front of the Ladrum bungalow. When Bambi grew big enough and became steady on her feet, she and Asha would run around the lawn every evening. It became a daily ritual, and it was such a joy to watch the two animals, one a domesticated one and the other straight out of the jungle, chasing each other up and down the lawn. When Bambi was full grown, we decided to release her into the jungle for her to meet up with her own kind. Like Elsa in *Born Free*, Bambi was born free, and like Elsa, we felt she should live free. Just outside the bungalow, there was a field of tea on one side. A wide footpath ran about a couple of hundred yards through it, ending in a jungle of thick scrub dotted with some trees. A tall hedge marked the boundary of the bungalow garden, and a little iron gate set in the middle of it opened out on to the footpath. The gate was loosely strung with barbed wire, and a small animal could squeeze through the gaps without too much difficulty.

One evening, my wife and I took Bambi to the edge of the tea. I was carrying her, and with some trepidation I put her down where the scrub started. We watched with bated breath to see what she would do. She first looked at us, then towards the jungle, and took a few tentative steps into the scrub. Looking back at us one last time, Bambi disappeared into the scrub. We walked in silence back to the bungalow, hoping no harm would come to her. Sleep was difficult that night, and Susie confessed the next morning that she lay awake for a long time thinking about Bambi before finally dropping off.

The next evening, while we were sitting on the verandah after tea, we were astonished to see Bambi walking through the little gate and towards the bungalow. As usual, Asha was with us. She saw Bambi at the same time we did, and bounded forward to meet her. The two of them immediately started their old game of chasing each other around the lawn. Just before dusk, we took Bambi to the back of the kitchen and fed her some fruit. She ate it, and as it started getting dark, she left us and slowly walked towards the gate, went through it and disappeared. Thereafter, Bambi would appear every evening at the same time, play with the dog, walk to the back of the kitchen, partake of whatever offering was given her and leave us. It was unbelievable.

A planter friend got to hear of our pet jungle sheep. He rang and asked me one day if he could bring his little daughter over to see this rare phenomenon. I told him he was welcome. As the animal came at almost the same time every evening, I asked him to arrive about fifteen minutes before Bambi normally would. He came with his daughter at the scheduled time, and parked his car in front of the bungalow facing the garden gate. I got in, and the three of us sat watching the gate. Almost on the dot, as if keeping an appointment, Bambi arrived. The dog was also waiting for her and they started playing as usual. My friend couldn't believe his eyes. I had told him what the ritual was, and the jungle sheep did not disappoint us.

A couple of years later, as the No.2, the Board asked me to act for the General Manager when he went on furlough. I had to also move into his bungalow on Glenmary Estate. A junior Superintendent who came to act for me on Ladrum, moved into my bungalow with a large Alsatian dog which belonged to the General Manager. He had offered to look after the dog while its owner was away on leave. Three months later, when I returned to my post on Ladrum, we waited as usual in the evenings for our Bambi to come through the gate. She never did. We surmised that the Alsatian dog must have frightened her away. We could only hope that the dog had not harmed our pet in any way.

❖❖❖

Ranikoil division of Ladrum Estate teemed with all kinds of wildlife. At the bottom of the division, the tea yielded to a forest. When I was an Assistant, while supervising work on the division, I would slip into the *shola* to see what wildlife I might encounter.

Water was plentiful when the South-West monsoon was active. But with the onset of the dry weather from December onwards, water became scarce. In the *shola*, though, there was a natural spring in the middle of a path which led from where the tea ended to some habitations in which the local Malayalees lived. This little spring attracted all kinds of birds. The odd woman from the huts nearby would also be there collecting water in pots.

On one occasion, I crossed the spring to go over to the other end of the *shola*. Not a living creature was around. When I came back a little later, I saw something move on the path near the spring and stopped to look. There, in front of me, playing with each other, were two little leopard cat kittens. They were most exquisitely marked, and were quite the prettiest little animals I had ever seen. I was very close to the kittens, but they were either oblivious of my presence or didn't care. Suddenly, while I stood watching, a fully-grown leopard cat, the mother obviously, sprang up onto the path from below and stood facing me with fangs bared and ears pinned back, snarling and twitching the tip of its tail. It was so belligerent that I felt fear such as I had never experienced before. Fortunately for me, it chose not to attack but made some sort of low sound which the two kittens heard. They stopped playing and jumped down to where the mother cat came from. The mother herself followed them, and all three vanished out of sight. I was on that division for two years, but never once did I see them again, even though I went to the same spot several times. Leopard cats are nocturnal animals, and are generally not seen in the daytime. I was truly lucky to have seen them at least once.

I am allergic to cats and like to keep even domestic ones at a distance. I was not born so. As a little boy, I was wandering around in my wealthy grandfather's spacious garden once, when I came across a large, empty earthenware pot. I looked inside and saw two cute little kittens. They looked beautiful, and in my innocence I picked up one of them. The kitten was obviously terribly frightened, and while attempting to get away, it scratched one of my forearms very badly and drew a lot of blood. I left cats strictly alone ever after that.

❖❖❖

Cobras were peculiar to Ranikoil division situated at an elevation of about three thousand five hundred feet above sea level, although the other divisions in the Company were only a few hundred feet higher. In Ranikoil too, cobras were generally encountered at the bottom of the division where the elevation was considerably lower than elsewhere. But in the dry weather especially, they could also be seen near the bungalow. There was a water tap just outside the bathroom of the bungalow, and a *Spathodia* tree grew close by. This moist and cool haven provided respite from the heat. One afternoon, after our son's ayah had gone away for her afternoon's rest, my wife opened the door of the bathroom leading out to rinse a couple of baby clothes under the tap. A cobra which had climbed onto the roof slipped and fell to the ground very close to her feet. Fortunately, Susie kept her cool and didn't move. After recovering from the shock of the fall, the cobra slowly slithered away.

On another occasion, my wife and I had adjourned to the sitting room after lunch, when suddenly our cook-butler rushed in. He was highly excited and hardly coherent. I caught the words *nalla paambu*. I asked him where it was, and he said just outside the kitchen. The kitchen in the Ranikoil bungalow stood by itself, a common feature in most of the homes built in the days of the British. An open passage led from the kitchen to the dining room. Although set apart, it was possible to see the kitchen from a side window in the dining room. I grabbed my .22 rifle from the adjacent bedroom, loaded it hastily, and rushed to the dining room window. Sure enough, there was a large cobra gliding along the outer wall of the kitchen. I quickly put the rifle to my shoulder and fired before the cobra could turn the corner of the kitchen wall and disappear. By great good fortune, my shot hit the cobra's spine. It just lay there writhing, and I dispatched it with a couple more shots.

I came across cobras on two other occasions. Once I was on my motorcycle coasting down a mossy cycle path in the tea when I suddenly saw a cobra in the middle of the path, a little distance away. I knew from past experience that if I braked suddenly on a mossy path, I would go for a spill, so I gently applied the brake and came to a halt very close to the cobra. It put its hood up, and the two of us had an eyeball to eyeball confrontation which lasted perhaps a minute but it seemed like much longer. No cobra will attack you unless it is provoked. This one was no exception to the rule. After what seemed an eternity, it quietly put its hood down and took off into the tea.

The last time I saw a cobra at close quarters was when I was on foot. Right at the bottom of the division, a lorry road was being cut on contract. One warm afternoon, when not much work was taking place, I took the contractor down to inspect the portion he had completed before passing it for payment. I was walking slightly ahead of him, but stopped when I saw a cobra sunning itself at the bottom of the road. Thinking the contractor was still following me, I put my right hand out behind me and asked him in a low voice to hand me a stone. Nothing happened. Slowly, I turned my head to see why the contractor hadn't obeyed me. He had seen the cobra before I did, and was standing some distance away with his eyes bulging and his mouth open. I could do nothing but stand transfixed where I was. The cobra had by now also seen me. It flicked out its tongue once or twice, and after a little while, slowly slid away. Although there were cobras on this division, and others must also have chanced on them, there was never a case of snakebite.

Even if they were not too plentiful, tigers were around in the 1950s. One day when I was attending evening muster, the Conductor on Ranikoil told me there was a tiger kill very close to my bungalow. The clerk on Ladrum Estate who owned a single-barrel shotgun had wanted to know if he had my permission to sit up for the tiger. I had no objection, so the Conductor sent someone to the clerk to convey my consent. There was still at least an hour of daylight left.

A motorcycle path connected the bungalow and the main road which led to the estate and factory. About fifty yards from the bungalow gate, along this path, was a nullah. Beside the nullah and just above the path, there was an *Albizzia* tree. *Albizzia* trees are large with thick smooth trunks and branches about fifteen or twenty feet from the ground. They are grown for shade in the tea fields, and this was a fairly large tree. The tiger kill – a worker's cow that had been grazing in the tea – was almost below the tree.

The next evening after muster I asked the Conductor if the clerk had sat up for the tiger the previous night and with what result. He said the clerk had proposed to sit and wait for the tiger in the *Albizzia* tree but found he could not climb it. Defeated, he had returned empty-handed.

Here was my chance to bag a tiger I thought. My uncle, Pandiaraj Davidar, was the Manager of a large estate about ten miles away, and he was a keen *shikari*. He had shot his tiger on Warwick Estate in The Nilgiris when he was the Manager there. As a boy, I had accompanied him on various shikar trips, and had seen him shoot all sorts of game, even a crocodile. In those days, you could shoot practically anything without having to worry about game laws. I got on my motorcycle and sped to his estate. He was in his bungalow. I told him about the tiger kill, and asked him if he could lend me his big-game rifle for the night. He gave it willingly, and also supplied me with some ammunition and his five-cell torch, saying I would need it.

I got back to my division well before nightfall. As there was no question of trying to climb the *Albizzia* tree which had thwarted the clerk the evening before, I had another plan. There was no electricity in the labour lines, and with no diversion of any kind, the workers usually had their supper early and went to bed. By about nine o'clock there was not a light anywhere, and the stillness of the night had to be experienced to be believed. I had my supper early, and told my servants to put out all the lights and retire for the night.

I sat and waited for some time. When I was certain that nothing moved on my division, I picked up the rifle, carefully loaded it and walked out of the bungalow and along the path. My plan was to move noiselessly up to where the kill was, shine the torch on the tiger which I hoped would be there, and shoot it with one well-placed shot as it looked down on me. If the tiger had not arrived, I was going to wait on the path about a hundred yards away, and hope to see it when I returned after a spell.

I switched on the torch as I came abreast of the kill. The tiger was not there. I had hardly gone a few yards when the foolhardiness of my action hit me. The tiger, if it had indeed been on the kill which was on higher ground, would had have a tremendous advantage over me. Angry at being disturbed, all it had to do was to take a leap and land on top of me, damaging me very severely or killing me before I could even put the rifle to my shoulder. I went cold all over. I quickly retraced my steps and heaved a sigh of relief when I reached the safety of my bungalow.

I have never seen a tiger in the wild. I have been told it can be a frightening experience. Horrocks once told me a tale of his own tryst with a tiger. When he had joined my Company as an Assistant in 1923, tigers were apparently very common. There was a tiger kill on his estate close to the tea, and a tree most conveniently overlooked the kill. Some men on the estate put up a *machan* or tree house and persuaded Horrocks to sit over the kill. As Horrocks had no gun of his own, one would suppose it was again the General Manager Wilkie's gun (with which he had shot a cow before) that he had borrowed for the job. The estate *shikari* sat by his side with a torch. The tiger did indeed turn up, and the *shikari* switched on the torch. The tiger looked up. As the *shikari* urged Horrocks to fire, the tiger bared its fangs and snarled. It unnerved Horrocks so much that in his fright he dropped the gun to the ground. That was the only time Horrocks aspired to bag a tiger.

One more tiger story and I will be through. Mir Nasir Ali Khan was the first Indian Assistant to be employed in TTE. Nasir, as he was popularly known, came from Hyderabad. He lived for shikar and would go wherever he heard an animal was sighted and shoot it.

At the time of this story, Dick Walters, the other Assistant in the Company, came to live in the Woodlands bungalow that I had vacated when I was posted out. The *shola* behind the bungalow went vertically uphill for a hundred yards or so before opening onto grassland. Michael, the hospital attendant, thought he saw or heard a tiger in the grassland one evening while collecting grass for his cows. Knowing about Nasir and his penchant for shikar, Michael went across to Nasir's estate and reported what he suspected. Nasir wasted no time, and came over the next evening after work. Michael accompanied him. Dick was at home that evening, and when he heard about Nasir's mission, he decided to tag along.

The three of them set off, up the hill, on the only footpath that ran through the *shola*. Dick led the way, Nasir followed and Michael brought up the rear. As they cleared the *shola*, Nasir slowed down and looked for signs of tiger pug marks on the ground. When they had gone some distance, Nasir happened to look up and was surprised to see Dick, who was ahead, running down the hill at great speed with his mouth open. As he drew near, Nasir asked, "What, Dick?" Dick managed to utter just one word, "Tiger." He then proceeded downhill at the rate of knots, and didn't stop until he reached his bungalow.

Alerted, Nasir now went up the hill cautiously. He hadn't gone very far when he saw the tiger, standing and looking at him within range of his rifle. The tiger was perhaps mystified

at the sudden disappearance of the white apparition that had
been there just moments before, and with the unexpected
appearance of this other human being the next instant. The
evening light was beginning to fade rapidly as it can do in the
hills. Nasir took careful aim and fired. The bullet found its
mark, and Nasir saw the tiger dropping where it stood. Before
he could walk up to the dead tiger, Nasir heard the loud roar
of another tiger close to where he had just shot the first one.
As twilight was giving way to night, Nasir decided that with
another tiger close by, discretion was the better part of valour,
and that he would come the next day to inspect the dead tiger.
As he turned to walk down, a comical sight met his eyes. On
hearing the shot and the simultaneous roar of a tiger, Michael
had leapt up and caught the lowest branch of the nearest tree,
and was clinging on for dear life, his feet barely above the
ground. Nasir went across to Michael and told him that the
tiger was dead, and asked him to let go of the branch. Michael
refused, so Nasir had to literally pull him down. Both of them
then hurried to the Woodlands bungalow to meet Dick. Dick
explained why he had behaved as he did. As he was trudging
up the hill, he saw this large animal which he thought was a
cow, and continued to walk towards it. And then it happened.
The animal kept watching Dick heading in its direction with
impunity, then decided to act. It opened its mouth and snarled.
That was when Dick realized it was not a cow but the tiger
itself, and took off down the hill in great haste.

Nasir went to have a look at his tiger the next day. He found
it had been partly eaten and the pelt was, therefore, of no value.
He came away leaving the carcass where it lay. Nasir left the
district for good a few years later, and until I retired and left
some fifteen years on, I did not hear of a single tiger being
shot by anybody in the district.

Directors' Foibles

Once a year, usually at the end of the calendar year, one of the Company Directors visited the estates to see if all was well. It was said that they chose that time of the year because it coincided with winter back Home, and gave them a chance to spend a little time in a warmer clime.

The first Director I met was Mr HL Pinches. Nobody told me anything about him. He was small-made and very pleasant. On his visit to Peermade, he came up to my bungalow, walked round it, complimented me on a couple of things and left.

Four years later, I met him again in London. He invited me to lunch with him at the famous Oriental Club just before I left for India after two months in England. I was only a junior Assistant and he needn't have bothered. He came all the way from his home in Eastbourne to take me to lunch. The previous day, I had gone to my Company's office to bid farewell to the Chairman, Col Williams, but he said I could say goodbye to him at the lunch hosted by Mr Pinches, as he would be there too. After lunch, Col Williams took his leave and Mr Pinches asked me if there was anything that I would like to say to him privately. I told him I had no problem really, except for a certain unease concerning my pay about which I had already spoken to the Chairman. He smiled and said, "Surely, you can also tell me about it, can't you?"

My pay was increased every now and then on an ad-hoc basis. I wanted it to be made a little more regular so that I would feel more secure. At the end of four years' service, although I was going to receive a fairly large increase in my salary, the difference between my pay and that of the only other Assistant, a European, which had also been increased, was somewhat disproportionate. I made it clear that I fully appreciated the fact that a man who came out from England should be paid more than someone living in India, but that I would only like the difference to be kept the same, as I felt that would be just and equitable. He merely said he understood, and we parted company on a warm note. Sometime later, after I returned to Peermade, I was informed by the General Manager that my salary was being raised further as directed by the Board. I found that my pay henceforth would be the same as that of the European Assistant. This adjustment was academic, as the European Assistant became an acting Superintendent shortly afterwards on a much higher scale of pay. But I couldn't help feeling that it was at the instance of Mr Pinches that I was shown the favour I had received. He wanted justice to be seen to be done. Though I never saw the great man again, I kept hearing about him. He went blind towards the end of his life, as did Madden. I can't think why blindness struck them, but they had both worked in the hills of Travancore.

It was while doing some research prior to starting on this book that I discovered what an extraordinary individual Mr Pinches had been in tea planting circles. Herbert Lloyd Pinches was the General Manager of the Kanan Devan Hills Produce Company (KDHP) in Munnar, one of the largest planting interests in the country, for eighteen years from 1911, and under his stewardship the Company scaled great heights. He initiated many schemes including The Munnar Valley Electric Works which produced power that was used in nine different factories, an achievement hitherto unknown. Munnar is now famous as a tourist destination. Pinches had also made his Company's Kanan Devan Tea very popular. When I was a boy of about ten in the 1930s, I remember seeing Kanan Devan Dust Tea in Trichinopoly. It was sold in little orange packets with the picture of a plucker on them. These packets of tea were bought every week in my grandfather's house, for what purpose I don't know because we were all coffee drinkers, unless it was given to the servants. But I never saw them taking a tea break.

By the year 1924, when everything seemed to be running smoothly, there was a cataclysm. The South-West monsoon arrived later than usual, and the rainfall it brought broke all previous records. Raging torrents of water rushed down the hillsides at ferocious speed, and unimaginable damage was caused. (I remember Horrocks recalling the devastation in Peermade which, like Munnar, suffered equally badly. A mile and a half of road on the way to Mundakayam had been washed away, and it was seriously debated if an earthquake had struck.) When it was all over, Pinches surveyed the havoc wreaked by the monsoon. It seemed that all the good work that he had done was irrevocably lost. Any other man in his position would have thrown up his hands in despair, but not Pinches. He was made of sterner stuff. Instead of admitting defeat, he got to work. Supported by loyal workers who would do anything for this remarkable man, he cleaned up everything, and in an extraordinarily short time, life on the estates was back to normal. Coincidentally, he was the Chairman of UPASI that same year and had other work to do besides managing the Company.

No one who saw Pinches, who seemed so mild, would know what a great man he was. For all his amazing achievements, he was the epitome of humility, and I was grateful for the privilege of knowing him.

I had been with the Company for about two years, when the Chairman, Col Williams, came on a visit. I was then the Assistant Superintendent on Ranikoil. Richardson was acting as the Superintendent of Ladrum Estate because Horrocks was away on furlough. The Chairman went round my division one afternoon, then came with Richardson to my bungalow for tea. After tea, Col Williams asked me if there was anything I would like to talk to him about. I was not too well paid, and found it difficult to make ends meet. Even after a couple of years of service, I had not been put on a regular scale of pay, and the Company's Board didn't seem to be even aware of what my salary was. Sometime after I joined, my General Manager informed me that my annual increment would be twenty five rupees a month – the amount paid to a European Assistant in the Company thirty years earlier, at which time, to quote Horrocks again, "Scotch whisky cost six rupees a bottle and English gin, five rupees." Since he appeared to be so friendly, I decided to tell Col Williams about my financial plight. As I started to speak, Richardson, who was also present, sensing what I was about to tell the Chairman, discreetly left the room and went into the garden, and remained there. Being the only Indian Executive in the Company was advantageous as no precedent in the matter of what my salary should be had been established. So, as tactfully as possible, I mustered the courage to appeal in Oliver Twist fashion, "Please, Sir, can I have some more pay?" He gave me a patient hearing, as they say, but didn't commit himself one way or the other.

I didn't think anything would come of my representation, and put it out of my mind. But I was glad to have got the matter off my chest. A few weeks later, I received a letter from the General Manager to say that my pay was to be increased forthwith by one hundred rupees a month on instructions from the Company's Board. It was a substantial increase in my relatively impoverished state. To get a salary increase of that sum would have taken four years of service in the normal course. A couple of days after I received Madden's letter informing me of my windfall, I met him on the road one afternoon when riding my motorcycle to the estate factory. He was setting out to attend a committee meeting of the District Planters' Association, and stopped his car to chat to me. At the end of our conversation, I thanked him for his letter conveying the news of the increase in my pay. He said abruptly, "You can thank the Chairman this time," put the car in gear, and drove away. I didn't know that he was miffed that I took my problem directly to the highest authority. Richardson told me later that the Chairman had spoken to him about my request, and that he, Richardson, had advised him that if the Company did not pay me properly, they would lose me. Which, theoretically at least, was eminently possible. Some of the other sterling Companies, and the rupee Companies manned by Europeans, had been sitting on the fence thus far, and they knew that sooner or later, they would also have to employ Indian Executives. And they were seriously interested in the hard-working Indian, which I certainly was, right on their doorstep. The No.1 of another Company once mentioned to me a figure which was much higher than what I was getting as salary one day when I met him on the road. The hint was more than obvious. He also invited me to visit him in his bungalow but I never did. My loyalty to my employer was too strong to be tempted by mere lucre.

I can still recall the time at the Peermade Club when I asked a very senior planter, AB (Andrew Boyd) Spence, the Group Manager of The Peermade Tea Company, a rupee Company that was managed by British planters, if I could give his name as a reference when I was applying for an outside job. Spence, a generous man, not only readily assented, but went further to suggest that if I was unhappy in my Company, I could always apply to his. I said that I wanted to quit planting, but asked him at the same time if it wouldn't look odd to leave my Company and join another in the same district. "Not at all," he replied. "Your fellow started in my Company, but when he thought that his chances of promotion were better in your Company than in mine, he left my Company to join yours. So, there you are." Madden's contemporaries, with whom he was not exactly popular, referred to him as 'Your fellow' in their conversations after they came to know me well.

By the time I became the Company's General Manager in India, my wife and I had entertained all the Directors in our home. After visiting an estate, it was usual for the Directors to spend the next day with us to rest and write up their report on that estate. They would also narrate any interesting incident they had experienced. In fact, when Col Williams learnt that I was retiring and leaving the Company's service, he wrote to me saying, "It was delightful having such close contact with a General Manager and his wife who really made us feel at home when visiting."

Col Williams had lost a leg in the Second World War and used an artificial limb. Everybody knew about it, but nobody referred to it except for this crude Assistant, whom I had the misfortune to recommend to the Board for appointment. He was known for his gaffes. When Col Williams went across to him for tea, he had asked, "They say you have a wooden leg, is it true?" The Chairman was a sport, and he had replied, "Of course, I'll show you," and proceeded to pull up his trouser leg to reveal his prosthesis.

Col Williams was a fitness freak, and went for long walks every day in spite of his disability. On his last visit, he arrived on a Saturday, while his official duties were to start only on Monday morning. So, on Sunday morning after breakfast, he suggested that we go for a walk. I took him straight up the hill on the wide lorry road behind the bungalow. When I thought we'd had enough, I decided to bring him back through a tea field, and we walked on the footpath the workers used. I led the way. As we came round a bend, I saw that a tree had fallen across the path, and the trunk was at least a foot above the ground. Involuntarily I said, "Oh". Col Williams who was right behind me heard me exclaim, and saw why I had done so. "Don't worry," he said reassuringly, "this leg of mine will take me where yours can go."

On another occasion, John and another Director who had worked as a planter in Malaysia, came out at the same time which was rather unusual. John declined to go round the estates which was the normal practice, saying that he had come to discuss Company matters with me, and stayed with us throughout the visit. The other Director, therefore, had to go it alone. But when it came to visiting the Assistant who'd embarrassed Col Williams, John offered to accompany his friend to his house for tea. They came back in a fit of temper and asked me how we could employ a man like that. For a start, they recounted, when they arrived at his bungalow, the man came out to receive them with his fly open. When these two Directors came out to India, there was not even a hint that the Company might be sold. There were probably rumours, but rumours were always floating around. But this chap wanted to get his facts right as he did with the Chairman and his artificial leg. Apparently, the table was spread with all kinds of things to eat. Just as they got started, the fellow had queried, "Is it true that the Company is going to be sold?" In an attempt to distract him, one of the Directors picked up an eatable from the table, took a bite and said, "Ah, this is nice, what do you call it?" They said it was most awkward all the time they were with him, and it was all they could do to keep the man from probing. They were most glad when the tea session came to an end.

Sometimes, the Directors would create trouble for themselves. On one of his visits, when I was the Superintendent of Kuduakarnam Estate, the Chairman wanted to meet the subordinate staff individually and informally, obviously with the best of intentions. He desired that they supervise work close to the road, so that he could stop by for a chat.

I was taking Col Williams around in the car as usual, and we first came across the Conductor of the division. He wore a planter's hat and was not exactly fluent in English. And, he was probably nervous to boot, meeting the Company's Chairman. I introduced him to the Chairman who said cheerily, "Ah, it's nice to be back." The Conductor lifted his hat by the crown with his left hand and said, "Yes." "Mr Davidar tells me you are doing good work." "Yes," he replied, and again he lifted his hat with his left hand. "I understand you are going to have a good crop this year." "Yes," the hat went up again by the crown. He seemed to have just this one affirmative word in his entire vocabulary on that particular morning.

The conversation with the Conductor was getting no where, so we proceeded on our way. One of the men the Chairman met had served in the Indian Army during the War. Knowing that the Chairman was also an ex-Army man, he became quite voluble and started telling the Chairman all about his life in the Army. He was an exception. Practically all the others had very little to say. One man was almost completely speechless and his eyes popped. The Chairman went through his stock comments, and by the end of his visit, he turned to me and said, "One doesn't quite know what to say to these chaps, you know." Needless to say, he didn't want the experience to be repeated on his subsequent visits.

Then there was the time when a Director who had the reputation of being a gourmet came on his visit. On the first evening, my wife, Susie, who normally would have supervised the cooking, said to me that she was suffering from a migraine, and had to take to bed. She was plagued by this malady during much of her life, and I have seen her completely prostrated when she had one of her severe attacks. This was one such occasion. I went to the kitchen and told the servants to pull out all the stops, and explained to the Director why my wife couldn't be with us that evening.

Not knowing what was in store, I did what I thought would help to get through the evening without incident. I plied the Director with large pegs of whisky – he was also known to be partial to alcohol – and I also helped myself liberally. As the spirits started taking effect, we swapped stories, and by the time dinner was announced, we were almost on backslapping terms.

This Director was originally a planter in Ceylon, and later became the No.1 of the Agency that eventually became the Managing Agents of my Company. He had spent some years in Coonoor, and one of the stories he told me was about the occasion he had to travel by train on business from Mettu-palayam, the railhead of The Nilgiris, to Madras. He found to his horror that his only travelling companion in the First Class compartment was a former Chief Minister of the erstwhile Madras State. This man led an austere life, and was known to be a typical Gandhian which stood for, among other things, someone who abstained from alcohol.

The Director had to have his sundowners. He wasn't sure if his fellow passenger would approve of his drinking. Anyhow, when the train started the sun had long set, so he took out his bottle of brandy and said to his companion, "Sir, I hope you don't mind my having a peg of brandy but I take it on my doctor's advice." The man who came from the deep South where drinking toddy was commonplace, replied with an absolutely straight face, "Not a bit, I'll have one with you." Could there have been a better way to break the ice?

Despite the initial hiccup of my wife's absence that evening, the meal passed off without any serious problem, and the rest of the visit went well too. So well in fact, that when the Director wrote to thank Susie for her hospitality, he said, "I was very comfortable and I know you must have given a lot of thought to the delicious meals you provided – you gave me all the things I like best.....I enjoyed our peaceful evenings when we discussed many subjects and had some good laughs together.....Thank you both very much for you hospitality – it made me feel more like a member of the family than an official visitor and that is the best hospitality one can wish for."

My final encounter with Directors was when John came to look for Indian partners a year before I retired. The day after we landed in Bombay, John met with some people, and that night another Director of the Company's Secretaries flew in from Malaysia (formerly Malaya) where he had been on an official visit. John and I went to meet him at the airport. The next morning, John announced that he had completed the job for which he had come, and said it was to be a fun day because they had to fly Home only late that night. He suggested we visit the Elephanta Caves, as the man who had chalked out his Indian itinerary had told him about this place. It was nothing short of amazing. It was also easy to reach the Caves because we just had to get in a motor launch at the Gateway of India opposite the Taj Hotel where we were staying. For the rest of the day, we just lazed about.

After dinner that night, we still had a lot of time to kill before setting out for the airport at midnight. The other Director, who was also youngish like John, said to me that he had heard about the red-light district in Bombay where the prostitutes entertained their customers in what were known as 'cages'. He asked seriously if we could go and see these women. I could see that John was embarrassed but he didn't say anything. I had passed through Bombay on several occasions, and had also heard about the notorious red-light district, but never felt inclined to go there.

Since the man seemed very keen, I told him I'd see if a ride there could be arranged. I went out of the hotel followed by the two Directors to speak to the driver of the car which had been laid on for our use by a Company in Bombay. I had a problem. The man, who was a local, spoke Hindi besides his own language, Marathi. I did not know Marathi, and had not spoken Hindi since I left the Army, all of twenty three years earlier. However, I managed to string together a few words that I remembered, and told the driver that the Sahibs wished to visit the red-light district in Bombay, and would he take us there, please? The man was naturally aghast. I quickly added, "*Sirf dekhna hai, karna nahin* (only to see, not to do)." Visibly relieved, he agreed to drive us there.

It was a sordid spectacle. The women were obviously not allowed any form of human dignity. I sat in front with the driver, and the two Directors occupied the back seat. The Director whose wish it was to visit this area, sat on the edge of his seat and soaked in the sight with great relish, while John, a devoted family man, whose close-knit family I had met, cowered in his corner but, nevertheless, took it in all the same. The Director who desired to see the 'exhibition' was of the opinion at the end of our 'tour' that it was the highlight of his trip to the East.

That was the last time I met any Director of the Company in India while in the Company's service, and I am not quite sure if it was a fitting finale.

～

On Two Wheels and Four

At the time I joined my Company, the roads within the estates and in the district were in quite good condition, and, consequently the bungalows of the planters were more easily accessible, even if the distances between them were generally great. The motorcycles and motor cars in the district were owned by the planters. There was a wide variety of machines. As imports were still allowed, the cars came from abroad. There were Vauxhalls, Austins, Standard Vanguards and other makes. In my own Company, there was a Ford Custom Sedan, two Standard Vanguards and a Hillman Minx. It was the same with the motorcycles. There were many incidents involving motor vehicles, some of them hilarious.

In motorcycles, as far as I know, the gear lever has to be depressed downwards to change to a higher gear. But, apparently, there was this one make of motorcycle – the name eludes my memory – in which you had to do the exact opposite in order to move to a higher gear. Richardson, my Superintendent and mentor as far as motorcycles were concerned, told me a funny story involving this kind of motorcycle.

There was a young Assistant who owned this motorcycle, and had yet to get used to the gear mechanism. Once when he was riding at some speed, he came to a field where some young pluckers were at work. He wanted to impress the lasses by going faster, which meant changing to a higher gear. Without thinking, he depressed the gear lever with his foot. It had the effect of braking suddenly, and he went over the handlebars, or to put it crudely and use a planter's expression, he went arse over tip, much to the great amusement of the pluckers.

Much the same thing happened to me once, but it had nothing to do with the gear lever. Woodlands division probably received the most rainfall in the Company during the South-West monsoon, and some fields on this division were also very heavily shaded with *Grevillea robusta* trees which meant that sunlight never penetrated to the earth in these places. Consequently, the roads were mossy and their surface smooth as glass. The pluckers were about their work in a field where the road was treacherous when I came along on my motorcycle. At about this place, I had once seen Richardson, an expert rider, come off his bike. The motorcycle fell on top of him, and the exhaust pipe burnt his right leg so badly that it took a long time to heal. On that occasion, I was behind him and managed to stop in time. So, this time around, I was extra careful. But in spite of it, I lost control at a slight bend in the road, skidded badly and fell off the bike. When you lose control on a mossy road, you really can't do much except hope for a soft landing. I was not hurt in any way, so I got back up on the bike and rode some distance. Thinking I would show the pluckers that I was not fazed by the mishap, I walked back to the field. It was a big mistake. Without exception, all the pluckers were holding their sides and almost crying with laughter. On seeing me, they stopped laughing. I had spoilt their fun.

Once again, on the same division, I was part of another incident though the workers were not involved. I had been with the Company for about three years, when it was decided to supply the Executive Staff with transport. Everyone got motorcycles, generally green Francis-Barnett machines. In addition, the Superintendents were provided with cars – Standard Vanguards initially, and later Ambassadors when the import of foreign cars was discontinued. By this time Dick Walters had arrived from England as an Assistant, and he would come over to the Woodlands division every day to receive an orientation in tea planting from me. Fairly close to the labour lines, a cow would chase my motorcycle every now and then, so I told Dick about it, and warned him to be careful. He asked me what was the best course of action if the cow gave chase. "Open full throttle, I suppose," I said airily and forgot all about it. One afternoon many days later, I was riding ahead with Dick Walters following as usual. At about the spot where I would normally encounter the cow, a white man on a green motorcycle hurtled past me. As Dick sped away, I heard the cow snorting right behind me. I took my own advice and opened full throttle.

The Woodlands division muster ground was not far from the spot where the cow took such a dislike to men on motorcycles on the Glenmary Estate road. Across the estate road and above it, opposite the muster ground, there was a volleyball court that the workers used. Just a little before the volleyball court, a short cut led off from the estate road. As it reached the volleyball court, it veered sharply to the right, before climbing steeply uphill. The short cut must have been a footpath originally, but it was later developed into a motorcycle road. When the Assistant Superintendents were all Europeans, the Company supplied them with small Standard Ten motor cars. Chris Calver, who was then the Assistant on Woodlands division, widened the motorcycle road to accommodate his small car. The short cut reduced the distance from the Assistant's bungalow on Woodlands to the muster ground by at least one kilometre; a similar distance was saved to the Glenmary Estate office from the Woodlands bungalow. Besides which, it served as a means to get to the Peermade Club quickly from Glenmary and the other estates in the Company. Although very useful, the short cut had to be negotiated with caution. It was almost certainly never used by the bigger cars in the Company.

At the time of this story, Angus Cameron was the Superintendent of Glenmary Estate and I was the Superintendent of Ladrum Estate. Glenmary was the closest to the Peermade Club, and Ladrum, the farthest away. One Saturday night,

Angus and I were at the Club as usual, and both of us happened to be grass widowers at the time. As the night wore on, the other members left, and only Angus and I remained. Angus was most interested in India, and we didn't realize how late it was as we sat chatting at the bar. And imbibing, I suppose. At about midnight, we decided to go home. Both Angus and I drove Ambassador cars provided by the Company. Angus got into his car first and set off. I followed.

Angus seemed to be going at some speed, and I was not too far behind. The return journey to our bungalows from the Club usually took much less time because we were lit up. Angus got to the short cut, and I was horrified to see him take it, instead of the main road like we usually did. I had no choice but to follow him, if only to make sure that he didn't come to any harm. Half way down this road, an outcrop jutted onto the road. On an earlier occasion, when riding my motorcycle, I had come to grief against that rock, under the influence naturally. I was worried that Angus might hit it, but he negotiated it skilfully. The other real danger was the sharp corner to the left at the volleyball court. If he missed the turn and went straight ahead as he could easily have done, Angus would have taken off from the revetment that abutted the road on the side of the volleyball court with disastrous consequences, given the speed at which he was travelling. The planters had a saying that God protected drunks and children. Thus far, God was on Angus' side. When I got to the volleyball court, I was greatly relieved to see that Angus had successfully crossed that hurdle too.

My sense of relief was, however, short-lived. As I reached the main road, I was very surprised to see two beams of light shining on the eucalyptus trees above the road, some hundred yards away. It struck me then that the two beams were emanating from the headlights of a car that was somewhere in the tea below the road. My head, if it was a little fuzzy until then, cleared instantly. The car had to be the one that Angus was driving. As soon as I got to the spot where the car must have left the road, I braked hard, jumped out and raced through the tea, which being a hybrid variety was not too high. I reached the car in record time. It was anybody's guess how many times the car must have somersaulted, but miraculously, it was standing on all four wheels and pointed towards the road. Angus had got out quickly, and stood leaning against the car. I looked inside the car. The ignition was still on. I removed the key, switched off the headlamps, and helped Angus climb up to the road. Neither of us said a word to each other, and Angus came up quietly. We got into my car, and I drove to Angus' bungalow. As he got out, I told him to go in and get to bed, and that everything would be all right. I waited until I saw him enter his bungalow and shut the front door behind him.

I drove back to my own estate. On the way to my bungalow, I had to pass the estate factory. I stopped there, woke up the Tea Maker and told him briefly what had happened. I said I would go to the bungalow and change into old clothes, and by the time I returned in about half an hour, I wanted him to assemble together the tractor driver and the tractor, and two or three men with pruning knives. The Tea Maker had carried out my instructions to the letter. I told the tractor driver to meet me at the muster ground of Wooodlands division. I took the men with me in the car.

As I drove about a couple of hundred yards beyond the Glenmary Estate gate, I was shocked to see Angus sitting on his motorcycle by the side of the road in utter darkness. I got really angry. I shouted at him and demanded, "Didn't I tell you to go to bed?" He was most contrite and pleaded, "Eddy, don't get angry. There is an expensive machine down there, somewhere in the tea, and you ask me to get to bed and go to sleep?" He was at least a mile from where the 'expensive machine' went down. I told him to leave the bike where it was, and get in my car. We then proceeded to where his car was in the tea. I parked my car with the lights shining in the direction of the car that had gone off the road, and instructed the men to use the pruning knives to cut the tea as low as possible in order to prepare a path for the car to be brought up. I made Angus sit on a culvert nearby, and told him not to move from there. He obeyed, as I could see him light up a cigarette from time to time.

The work was slow but steady and the torch I had brought with me from the bungalow helped. Just a short while before dawn, a rough path was ready. I got into the car that was in the tea and told the tractor driver to slowly winch the car forward. To my great joy, the car gradually moved up the hill, and we reached the road rather quickly. I asked Angus to get in his car and drive slowly, and said that I would be right behind. His head more than clear by now, Angus did as he was told.

As dawn broke on Sunday morning, I reached my own bungalow and slept for most of the day. Angus Cameron was most grateful. To show his appreciation, Angus presented me with *The Swinging Safari* by Bert Kaempfert, a long-playing gramophone record from his record collection. It was a new release, and he knew I loved to listen to its catchy beat. I still have that record with me.

Not everyone who went to the Club got home the same night. Horrocks went to the Club one Saturday evening, and when returning rather late, thought the road didn't seem too familiar. He drove around aimlessly for a while, then decided to go to sleep in the car, and get his bearings the next day. When he woke up in the morning and looked around, he found he was barely a couple of hundred yards from his estate gate.

I was Horrocks' Assistant on Ranikoil for about two years when Madden decided that I and the other Assistant in the Company should go down with Horrocks to Cochin to meet the Company's Tea Brokers for a discussion on how teas were valued and sold in the auctions. Horrocks wished to make an early start, so he asked us to have supper in our own homes, after which we were to go across to his bungalow to spend the night. My bungalow was less than ten minutes away, and I could easily have made it in good time, but Horrocks said it would help if all of us were in one place the night before we left for Cochin.

Horrocks had by this time bought himself a second-hand American Hudson car which he had always admired. It was long and sleek, and was called the 'boat' as it resembled one. I actually acquired it from him a couple of years later, with a loan from the Company. I am yet to drive a car that runs as fast and as smoothly as that Hudson.

The other Assistant and I arrived at his bungalow at the time indicated, but Horrocks himself was missing. Both of us sat around and smoked and chatted. After a considerable period of time, we decided to go to bed was we had no idea where Horrocks was. When we awoke in the morning, there was still no sign of Horrocks. We did our chores and got dressed, and presently, we heard a car driving up. It was the 'boat'.

Horrocks told us that he had gone to the Peermade Club the previous evening. It had been raining, and on his return, the car had slid into a drain by the side of the road in a neighbouring estate, and had got stuck. From previous experience, he knew how futile it would be to try and get the car out, and hence decided to spend the night inside it. We asked him how he managed to extricate himself from the drain in the morning. He simply said, "Horsepower of the East." The next day, apparently, the men on the estate were going to work and had found his car in the drain. They stopped by and helped to pull the car out.

I had a similar experience myself in the same Hudson. I decided one evening to visit my good friend, Eddie Taylor, who lived on an estate many miles away. We spent a pleasant evening together, and I left after dinner. Late at night, nothing moves on an estate road. It can be quite eerie but there is no danger from man or beast. I drove along serenely and passed a small township which was not too far from Glenmary Estate. Then I came to a fork in the road. Both the roads which branched off looked the same, and I took the one which I thought was the correct one. It kept getting narrower and when I couldn't proceed any farther, I discovered it was an estate road which culminated in a dead end. There was no question of reversing all the way back in the dead of night, so I went to sleep in the car, in Horrocks' fashion. I got back to my estate first thing in the morning.

Horrocks had a way with motor vehicles. He got himself an Austin-7 of 1937 vintage. The car would do just what he wanted, and he could get it to perform like a circus animal. One trick Horrocks showed me was to get the car to keep pace with him as he walked alongside. He started the car outside his bungalow, pointed it in the direction of the garage, put it in gear and got out. The car matched his walking speed and never stalled.

Madden would make rules for the Company as it suited him. Rather like Horatio Nelson, the British Admiral of Trafalgar fame, who said before the famous battle, "England expects every man will do his duty," Madden had decreed that all the Executives in the Company would call on the Maharaja of Travancore, Chithira Thirunal Balarama Varma, when he was in residence in his summer palace in Kuttikanam, the point of entry into Peermade, ten miles from Ladrum Estate. Anyone intending to meet the Maharaja was required to sign the Visitors' Book which was kept in a room at the entrance to the palace. Before long, they would be invited in batches to take tea with him.

Horrocks came to see me in the field one morning to say that Madden had telephoned to inform him that the Maharaja had come up to his palace in Kuttikanam. Horrocks wanted company, and suggested that I go across to his bungalow after tea, from where we could go together in his car to sign up. The arrangement seemed fine to me.

That evening, we got into his Austin-7 and set off for the palace. We chugged along at the stately speed of about fifteen miles an hour with the canvas hood down. As we neared the palace, we saw a group of people on the main road – with some policemen in attendance – approaching us on foot. At the head of the group, looking at us pointedly, was none other than the Princess, the sister of the Maharaja. She was probably curious to see who was coming her way in a car.

Returning after signing the Visitors' Book, we saw a *kutcha* (country) road leading from the side of the palace towards the main road. Horrocks suggested we take the *kutcha* road so as to avoid the Princess as she returned from her walk. We had gone less than a mile when we saw the Princess and her entourage coming down that very road. As we passed her, she gave us a broad smile as if to say, "Gotcha."

In due course, we were summoned to the palace. A couple of British planters and their wives, and some prominent local residents had also been invited. The Maharaja was slightly built but handsome and extremely vivacious. He spoke to everybody, and seemed to know everything about everything. Tea arrived. There were sandwiches and assorted snacks. As the sun went down, card tables were laid for bridge, and we were served a couple of pegs of whisky, Scotch naturally.

At the appointed time, we took our leave. I thanked the Maharaja, and turned to walk away. I had hardly taken a couple of paces when I noticed that the Indians, all Malayalees, were bowing to the Maharaja and were walking backwards. I promptly reversed direction. The Maharaja was vastly amused.

There was a lighter side to incidents featuring motor cars. I found one quite amusing when it took place. Madden had owned a Ford Custom Sedan which he sold to the Company, and my General Manager had the use of it as the No.1 of the Company when the General Manager and Superintendents were supplied cars by the Company. One night he was driving back alone from the Club, and had stopped on the road to take a leak. He had parked the car on a slope, and thinking that he had applied the hand brake as usual, he walked to the front of the car. Suddenly he felt something ram into him from behind, knocking him down. He realized with horror that it was his car, and watched as it slowly passed over him. Fortunately for him, the car had a high ground clearance. He lay still until the car cleared him, then got up quickly, ran after it before it gathered momentum, jumped in and brought the car to a halt.

I told the story to my children because I thought it was funny. My little daughter, Lulu, liked stories to have a proper ending. She asked me seriously, "Did he finish making soo-soo?"

Days and Nights at the Club

No planting district could ever be complete without a Planters' Club, and Peermade was no exception. The Peermade Club had once been an estate Manager's bungalow. It had character. The front hall with its wooden flooring was spacious, and was dominated by a massive and impressive head of a gaur, also known as the Indian bison, which was mounted over the fireplace. The bison looked down on the proceedings that took place in the hall, typically the Club meetings, and the meetings of the District Planters' Association, besides the Club dances.

The Peermade Club fostered a unique tradition. Planters retiring from the district parted with their planter's hats. They adorned the walls of the bar room and were part of the Club's memorabilia. By the time I became a planter, this practice had been discontinued, probably because most planters didn't don hats.

At the time of signing my agreement with the Company, Madden told me that I could have Saturday afternoons off because the planters and their wives generally met at the Club on Saturday evenings. I was duly made a member of the Peermade Club.

On the first two occasions, as dusk fell, my Superintendent, Richardson, and his wife took me to the Club in their Hillman Minx. Not many members were present, probably because the sporting season was over. The few members and their wives who were there sat around in a circle with a fire blazing away in the hearth, exchanging stories, mostly about their experiences in the United Kingdom. I sat silently sipping my drink until it was time to go home.

Meanwhile, my own motorcycle arrived from Madras, and I told Richardson that henceforth I'd make my own way to the Club. The South-West monsoon had set in by then, and brought with it drenching rain. I tried going to the Club on a couple of occasions on my motorcycle but arrived looking like a wet hen. In any case, I hardly participated in the ritual conversation, so I stopped going altogether until the days were bright and sunny again.

There was this amusing story of the young Scotsman who had recently become an Assistant on one of the estates in the district. Standing with the young man in the nursery of the division, the Visiting Agent or VA – typically an outsider paid to visit the estates and report on them – had asked, to put him at ease, "I understand you had rain last night. How much was it?" On every division, rain was measured in inches, but the Assistant was still attuned to life back Home. "Ooh, Sir, pints and pints," he replied. Not one to give up easily, the VA queried, "I see you have a lot of tea plants in your nursery. Do you have any idea how many there are?" The young chap said, "Ooh, Sir, thoosands and thoosands." At which point, the VA decided it was pointless to persist with eliciting answers from so new a recruit. A little digression but worth relating, I reckon.

On one occasion at the Club, three people intended playing bridge, and were looking for a fourth player. I was no Omar Sharif at bridge but I was not a novice either. In my last year in the Army, my battery was posted in Jammu where we lived in tents. Pakistan constantly threatened to attack us in those early days. As we could do nothing but wait, three other brother officers and I played bridge every night in the Mess tent to while away the time. So, that evening, when I was asked if I played bridge, I admitted I did.

I drew as my partner a small, quite good-looking woman. She must have been an attractive bit of stuff in her younger days. A senior planter told me that she did indeed attract men, especially men from outside the district. It was my first experience of playing bridge with white people, and I was a little apprehensive. My partner didn't help matters either. She had a querulous manner and a whiny voice, and as the game progressed, she kept repeating the expression one dreads to hear at a bridge table, "Oh, partner." The more she whined, the more mistakes I made. I probably hastened the end of the rubber, and was most relieved when it was all over and I could make good my escape.

As I got up, a tall, well-built man who had been standing behind me all the while, said, "Don't worry about that woman, she knows as much bridge as the man on the moon." Little did anyone know that sixteen years later, on 20 July 1969 to be precise, there would indeed be a man on the moon, if only for a short period of time. The first thing Neil Armstrong said when he set foot on the moon's surface was, as the whole world knows, "That's one small step for man but one great leap for mankind." After having made that momentous statement, he went on to say, "I'd like a glass of iced tea."

Neil Armstrong was an American, and typically, Americans prefer coffee to tea. It would be but natural to want to know how iced tea came into being. According to Gilles Brochard whose contribution appears in *The Book of Tea* edited by Anthony Burgess, a tea dealer by the name of Richard Blechynden went to the Saint Louis World's Fair in 1904 to introduce Americans to black tea from India. In the sizzling hot weather that prevailed, it was unlikely that the visitors could be tempted to partake of hot tea, so Blechynden, an enterprising American, put two ice cubes in a glass and poured tea over them. Iced tea was thus born. An interesting aside – Americans apparently drink a lot of iced tea with lemon and sugar but sometimes also laced with a little rum.

To get back to our story, the man who spoke so kindly to me was Henry Boone, a tea planter with TTE. He surprised me by saying, "I knew your cousin Major Victor during the War." My cousin ADJ Victor went on to become a Brigadier, and when he was posted in Trivandrum, he actually came to represent his Club in a bridge tournament held at the Peermade Club.

How did this man know I was Victor's cousin? I never got to find out. Henry Boone had obviously served in India, and having become attracted to the country, he'd returned to plant tea. He certainly didn't have to come to India to earn a living, as he was said to be independently very well off.

Every year, the dry weather ushered in the tennis season. The district had two planters' Clubs, the Peermade Club and the Vandiperiyar Club. We played tennis matches against each other. Henry Boone was the number one singles player of the Vandiperiyar Club, and the best in the district of Peermade-Vandiperiyar. He stood over six feet tall and was powerfully built. When I, representing Peermade Club, had to play against him, he usually demolished me. His service in particular, delivered from a great height, was almost unplayable. For me, at any rate.

After a few years in the district, Boone contracted a strange illness. It could not be cured locally, so he was sent back to England for treatment. He was admitted to the Hospital for Tropical Diseases in London, where he showed no sign of recovery and his illness continued to defy a diagnosis. Horrocks, who happened to be in London on furlough at the time, went to visit Boone in hospital. Boone's symptoms appeared vaguely familiar to him. Horrocks asked the doctor responsible for treating Boone whether they had considered relapsing fever, the mystery illness that his father, Dr O Horrocks, had diagnosed and successfully treated in a number of cases when he was the Chief Medical Officer in the planting district of Anamallais near Coimbatore in South India. Horrocks thought it most unfair when he was banned from visiting Boone thereafter.

We must dwell here a little on the life and times of Dr O Horrocks. Dr Horrocks had an FRCS (Edinburgh) degree, a prestigious degree by any standard. He secured a job as Medical Officer on the Nagda-Muttra railway construction in North India in 1905. Three years later, the family went back to England. Dr Horrocks became a General Practitioner (GP), and set up a practice in the United Kingdom. They lived on a farm in Kent which the good doctor owned. There were times when calls for help came in the middle of the night, and Dr Horrocks felt duty-bound to respond to them. He had a car, but he had to crank the engine to get it to start. On a cold night, needless to say, it took some time for the engine to come to life. That was when Dr Horrocks coined the slogan, 'Never be a servant of the public'.

In course of time, Dr Horrocks got quite fed up with the life he led in England. One evening, while sitting on a bluff overlooking the English Channel, he saw some ships sailing eastwards. That was when he vowed that he would board one of those ships to India some day and never come back. And, he did just that. According to his son, Oswald Horrocks, the family came out to India in 1922 when Dr Horrocks bought himself a house in Coonoor in The Nilgiris – I have actually seen it from the description Horrocks gave me about its location when we came to settle in Wellington. Dr Horrocks worked for some years as the Chief Medical Officer in the Anamallais, then retired to Coonoor where he lived until his death. He lies buried in the Tiger Hill Cemetery in Coonoor.

The Peermade Club came to life when the monsoon receded. Everybody who could play tennis turned up in tennis kit, not just those who competed in tournaments. I hadn't realized until then that going to the Club was such a pleasurable experience. I looked forward to Saturday afternoons. After tennis, we usually changed into grey flannel trousers and sports jackets, and sat around chatting. By an unwritten code, shop talk was taboo. Gradually, I came to be accepted which was nice, and I no longer felt like a stranger in the Club.

Some of the older members – and I can think of one gentleman in particular – used language which must be peculiar to the Peermade Club. The Club Writer's Assistant was a young fellow called Pillay. When ordering his drink, this gentleman would say to Pillay 'coming, running, jumping' to hasten its arrival at the table.

Spence was a regular at the Peermade Club. He would arrive as the sun was setting every Saturday evening, always dressed in grey flannel trousers, blue blazer and a striped tie. The bar room had three small tables. Spence would sit at one of them the whole evening, but not before removing his blazer and carefully draping it over the back of his chair. He drank whisky – Scotch if there was any – and smoked Three Castles cigarettes which came in a tin with a greenish-coloured label, the most expensive cigarettes available at the time.

Spence was a bachelor, and allowed India to spoil him thoroughly. His cook-butler would fill his cigarette case every morning and hand it to him when he left for the field after breakfast. Once a month, he would pay his Club bill by cheque. From where he sat, he would summon Pillay. When Pillay got to his table, he would instruct, "Put your hand in the left pocket of my coat, and you will find my chequebook. Take it and fill one leaf with the amount of last month's Club bill, and bring it to me for my signature." Pillay would do as he was ordered. Spence would then tell him to tear off the signed cheque and replace the chequebook in the same pocket.

Some of Spence's young expatriate friends were worried that he would find living in England by himself difficult after retirement. He usually stayed in his Club when he went Home on furlough, and played golf regularly there. His friends thought that his money would not last very long if he took up residence in his Club when he left India for good. They felt he would be able to manage fairly comfortably if he retired to Coonoor in The Nilgiris where he would be in demand as a VA, as a European VA was preferred by Indian companies.

Spence didn't live too long after he retired to England after forty years of planting. He died in England of an aneurysm of the aorta at the age of sixty.

I heard from Horrocks that there was an unusual visitor to the Club in 1926. It was none other than Somerset Maugham, the famous writer, who had come to the Club one evening at the age of fifty two. Maugham was one of my favourite authors, and I had read most of his books (*Of Human Bondage* being one of his best), and practically all of his short stories. Many of his short stories featured planters and their way of life, and he was generally not complimentary to them.

I was quite excited to learn about Maugham's visit and wanted to know what he said or did. Apparently, he spoke to no one but just sat quietly watching the people in the Club, almost certainly gathering material for some of his future stories.

In 1971, the Peermade Club celebrated its Golden Jubilee, and there was just one European member left, named perhaps most appropriately, Victor Whyte. The other European planters had either retired or left after resigning their jobs for one reason or the other. I soon found that as a senior member I had very little in common with most of the other members of the Club. Shop talk which was once unthinkable crept in. I once heard a planter tell his buddies about some labour trouble. "Those fellows don't know about me. Don't worry, I'll fix them yet," he bragged. And to think that we went to the Club to forget about labour trouble. Most of the young chaps were innocent of the reading habit, and it was difficult to engage them in conversation. After a while, I stopped going to the Club altogether.

It so happened that I later resigned my Club membership over a matter of principle. That act must have been unheard of, and unprecedented. Neither did I miss the Club, nor daresay I, did anyone miss me. I didn't know at the time that I would be leaving the district shortly. Even though I was not a member of the Peermade Club when I retired, the Club Committee sent me a crystal vase as a farewell gift, for which most of the members had subscribed. I felt greatly honoured by their gracious gesture.

∾

Gentlemen's Gentlemen

It was PG Wodehouse, my favourite author, who conferred the appellation a gentleman's gentleman on the sagacious Jeeves, Bertie Wooster's manservant. Hence the chapter's title with due apologies to all of them.

When I was appointed an Assistant Superintendent in the Company, the General Manager sent me a letter containing various instructions. He clearly stated that although the Company would provide two bungalow servants, I should have my own personal servant. I took a man with me from Madras who would serve as my cook-butler. He was a smart fellow, who could cook both Indian and Western food very well. He also kept the house clean at all times.

Apart from his salary, he had all his meals in my house, and ate what I ate. As a bachelor, I could not keep an eye on him at all times, so he helped himself to whatever he could lay his hands on. He would bring me bills from time to time for purchases that he had made for the house. As I had no means of checking, I always paid up. Every Sunday morning, my cook-butler went to the local bazaar and returned before lunchtime. The bazaar was located a few miles away in a small township called Pambanar that adjoined Glenmary Estate. Before he left for the market, he would take ten rupees from me, which went pretty far in those days. In the evening, he would produce a detailed bill, listing all the items clearly. The total was always a few rupees more than the money I gave him. At the bottom he would clearly state, "Master give rupees three," or whatever. I paid without question. He took me for a sucker, and started cheating me in all kinds of ways. But I never minded because

I could afford the little extra money he took from me, and he always fed me well and kept the house neat and tidy.

The man was married with a little child. Unfortunately, the bungalow did not have any servants' quarters, only a small room adjoining the kitchen in which he could not have possibly kept his family. He had plenty of time to kill in the afternoons after I went to work, and he started to stray. There were two or three young wenches among the pluckers who were personable, and his eyes fell upon one of them.

As it happened, his movements were observed, and the Chief Clerk in the Head Office, a Tamil Christian like myself, who lived in a house not too far from mine but on another hill, came to see me one evening. He stood outside in the garden and engaged me in conversation. He spoke in riddles, and for much of the time, I couldn't understand what he was saying. And then, it dawned on me. He was cautioning me in a roundabout way about the dangers of getting mixed up with the women on the estate. He was probably under the impression that my cook was pimping for me. By and by he left, obviously convinced that he'd given me good advice.

Not long afterwards, I myself came to know about my cook's activities in his spare time. I summoned him and asked him if he was playing around with any woman on the estate. He, naturally, denied it. I was not aware that pressure was being applied on the man by the workers themselves, and probably by the close relations of the girl he had been interested in. One morning, I lay in bed and waited as usual for my morning cup of tea to be brought to me before I got on with my morning chores. It was not forthcoming. It was getting late, so I got out of bed and went to the kitchen to investigate. The kitchen was deserted, as the other worker who assisted in the kitchen, generally referred to as the kitchen coolie, wasn't expected yet. Then I saw a piece of paper lying on the kitchen table. My cook-butler had written me a letter, his farewell letter. He said that the shame of having false accusations levelled against him

was too much for him to bear, so he had decided to leave. I
was shaken. In a short while, though, the kitchen coolie arrived
and took charge in a limited sort of way.

My cook-butler must have planned his departure very
carefully, and I couldn't tell which of my belongings he had
helped himself to. Apart from what cash he could lay his hands
on, two valued personal possessions were evidently missing.
One was a gold ring with an emerald, my birthstone, that my
wealthy grandfather had presented me when I passed a
university examination several years previously. I never wore
it, but kept it in the button box on my dresser. The other was a
photograph of my first Battery Commander and me, both of
us in uniform. When I left the Army on being released, I went
to Amritsar from Jammu to say goodbye to my former Battery
Commander who was posted to a unit there. I thought it would
be a nice gesture, even if it meant taking a detour to Amritsar
before going to Madras, as we got on exceptionally well. He'd
said he would come to the station to see me off. On the way, we
had stopped at a photographic studio where he had previously
arranged for a photograph to be taken of both of us together.
He sent me the photograph later. It was a good picture, with
both of us looking smart in our uniforms, and I had kept it on
the sitting room mantelpiece. I had no doubt that my cook-
butler was using it to get further employment, in all probability
saying that he worked for Major Balbir Singh Rana, a Rajput.

The Sunday after my cook-butler abruptly left me, I asked
my garden coolie to go to the bazaar to buy the provisions
that were needed the following week. I gave him the bill last
submitted by my cook with instructions to buy the things that
were listed in it, and the necessary money.

My bungalow was situated on top of a hill, and a steep road
led straight up to it from the bottom. At about midday, I went
and stood at the gate and looked down. Everything was quiet
and peaceful. Presently, I saw a man with a big basket on his
head climbing up the hill. As he drew near, I realized he was

my garden coolie. I opened the gate for him. He walked past me and round to the back of the bungalow to enter the kitchen. As he was staggering under the weight of a rather heavy basket, I was curious to know what was in it. By the time I entered the kitchen, he had emptied the basket onto the large kitchen table. I was dumbstruck by what I saw. I asked him why he had bought such vast quantities of everything. He said simply that he had only bought what was in the list that I gave him. I had been gypped week after week.

The man who took the place of my departed cook-butler came from an estate at the other end of the district. He had been employed in the bungalow of a senior European planter as a travelling *chokra* (literally, a little boy), and went with his master on his travels to pack his bags and to look after his needs. But, he knew no cooking as I discovered soon after I employed him. Being the juniormost executive in the Company, I was sent wherever someone was needed to hold temporary charge, and, except for a fairly lengthy stay on one division, I was shunted around at frequent intervals. And as I moved from bungalow to bungalow, I was exposed to a medley of cooking talents, and the quality of my food varied with the ability of the bungalow's kitchen coolie.

My new 'cook' was into another kind of thieving. On the first day of every month, unless it was a Sunday, the fellow would come to me after breakfast with a list of my monthly household requirements. He found it only too easy to dupe me as I would write down everything he read out without asking any questions and sign it. He would then go to Spencer's and make the purchases. On the following day he would take a day's leave, ostensibly to visit his family. The garden coolie would accompany him as far as the nearest bus stop to help carry his bags – he was taking home most of the things he had bought the previous day on my account at Spencer's.

I learnt rather late that before he joined me, my cook-butler ran a small tea shop on the estate where he lived. Every month,

I was providing most of the supplies he needed for his shop. I remember the wife of a senior planter asking me once what I bought from Spencer's, and the quantities of items like sugar, American flour and such like. I replied twenty pounds each of sugar and flour, and some large quantity of cooking oil, among other things. She just said, "Oh," and kept quiet. Nobody warned me that I was being robbed blind, and I am not sure I would have done anything even if I had known about it. I had been hoping to get out of planting much of the time, so I wouldn't have bothered to sack him. Moreover, it would have meant having to look for someone else to replace him, and I didn't want to take the trouble. When I got married, the first casualty on the household front was, unsurprisingly, my cook-butler. One of the first things my brand-new wife did was to take charge of the storeroom. She put it under lock and key, and would dole out just what was needed for the kitchen every day. After nearly four years of unfettered freedom, the slight was more than the crooked fellow could bear. As he was also going to lose the income that he was making on the side, he gave notice and left a few days after my wife came to live with me. My monthly Spencer's bill also came down drastically after the thief left, as Susie made out the shopping list and sent one of the bungalow coolies to get what she needed.

I was not the only one to have problems with my cook-butler. The wife of a contemporary of mine was having problems too, despite the fact that she watched her cook-butler constantly with eagle eyes. His weakness seemed to be sugar, and she was forever accusing him of stealing it. One day she decided to get rid of him – he was not the first person she'd sacked for pilferage. The man took it quite well but asked her for a 'satpit', a certificate for his service as he was leaving. For some reason, it seemed to be the norm. One man whom we employed, and who stayed with us for several years, came with a handful of chits from his previous employers. Anyway, the good lady obliged her cook-butler.

The woman's husband was standing on the road watching some work that was going on, when his dismissed cook-butler came along. He stopped and showed his erstwhile master the certificate that the lady of the house had given him. Obviously, he had shown the certificate to someone who knew his English, as he pointed to one place in the chit and expressed his displeasure about what was written. His former master read it, and noticed that his wife had mentioned that the man had 'light fingers'. My friend thought quickly and said to the cook-butler, "You are good at making pastry, aren't you? That's what it says, that your fingers are light." Much to his relief, the man left, but it was anybody's guess whether he agreed with the explanation or not.

There was this other cook-butler who liked fresh eggs. When McIntyre went on furlough once, Richardson, as the junior Superintendent, acted for him. He and his wife Jean found that Mrs McIntyre kept some nice Rhode Island Red chickens for their eggs. Jean Richardson realized after some time that she was not getting any eggs, and came to the conclusion that someone was helping himself to them. So, the next time a hen cackled, she hastened to the chicken run and almost collided with her cook-butler who was also heading in the same direction. She told us that from that day onwards, she made it a point to be at the chicken run when she heard a hen cackle to announce the laying of an egg.

Eddie Taylor came from Aberdeen in Scotland. He worked as an Assistant Superintendent for a rupee Company run by British planters. He was the first one to befriend me in the Peermade Club during the early awkward days, and helped me feel, to some extent, less of an outsider. We were both bachelors at that time, and soon became friends. Eddie and I met most Sunday mornings in the Club, and he usually had a fund of stories to tell.

One day Eddie thought that his cook-butler's shirt looked familiar. He didn't say anything, and kept his suspicion to himself. Not long afterwards, Eddie had to change a fused light bulb. As it was out of reach, he got up on a table to replace it, and his cook-butler stood beside the table to hand him the new bulb. When Eddie looked down to take the bulb, he got a glimpse of the label inside the man's shirt collar. His suspicion was confirmed. The cook-butler was, indeed, wearing Eddie's shirt. Appearing to sound casual, Eddie asked, "Boy (by custom, the cook-butler of any age was called 'boy' on the estates), we shop in the same shop, do we?" The man replied, solemnly, "Yes, Master."

And then, there was this senior planter, Milne of Kotamullai Estate, who thought that the cigarettes in his tin were slowly disappearing. (In those days, cigarettes came in tins of fifty, besides the usual packets of ten.) His cook-butler was, naturally, the prime suspect.

Milne decided to lay a trap. One day, he carefully counted the cigarettes in his tin. He didn't take a cigarette from the tin that day, and when he counted them later, as expected, some were missing. He carefully removed the tobacco from the few cigarettes he was going to leave in the tin, put some gunpowder from one of his cartridges in the middle of each, then replaced the tobacco at both ends, packing it as tightly as possible. When finished, he put the tin back in its usual place. That night when his cook-butler served him and his wife dinner, he was pleased to see that the man's eyebrows were badly singed. His cigarettes were left untouched after that. Milne had a rare old time telling us the story in the Club in his Scottish burr.

Spence was a brilliant raconteur. I liked to sit at his table in the bar room of the Club and listen to his stories about his early days in planting. He had this story to tell. Each day at noon, he had a glass of lime juice cordial before lunch. The cordial, a jug of water and a glass were always kept ready by his cook-butler so that he could have his usual drink when he got back from the field.

Spence having developed acidity in his stomach, consulted a doctor about it. The doctor found that Spence drank lime juice cordial every day. He advised him to stop drinking the cordial for some time, as he felt it probably aggravated his condition. Spence took his advice, but refrained from telling his cook-butler that he did not want the lime juice cordial any longer. After a couple of days, he thought the level of the cordial in the bottle was less than before. So, he decided to watch it. Just as he thought, the level went down every day, as it would have had he been drinking it. One day when the cook-butler came to announce lunch, Spence confronted him with it. Spence told him that he himself hadn't touched the cordial for many days, and wanted to know who had been drinking it. The cook-butler denied all knowledge, and left the room. Soon, Spence heard loud noises emanating from the kitchen. His cook-butler and the kitchen coolie were having a heated argument, and Spence knew the cause of the row was his cordial.

There must be many more stories relating to butlers. But the general attitude among the planters was that the devil you knew was better than the one you didn't, even if it meant putting up with their unsavoury ways.

∽

A Question of Colour

The Board of my Company sent out the airmail edition of *The London Times* for its Executive Staff in India. I don't know how many of the others read it, but my wife and I highly valued this perquisite which was a hangover from the time when the planters and their wives were all British. Both *The London Times* and *The Daily Telegraph* were supplied at one time, but with the Indians coming in, *The Daily Telegraph* was discontinued. I can still recall the names of writers who appealed to me – Bernard Levin for his chaste English, and John Woodcock and Rex Bellamy who wrote columns on cricket and tennis respectively in the *Times*. My wife looked forward to reading the sections on gardening, Nature and food, among others.

In the *Times* issue of 16 May 1970, the following extract from *Stars of the Desert* appeared in an article: "Men should be judged not by their tint of skin, the Gods they serve, the vintage they drink, nor the way they fight or love or sin. But by the quality of the thought they think."

This appealed to me so much that I wrote to the newspaper to ask for further details of *Stars of the Desert*, as I wanted to read it in its entirety. The member of the newspaper staff who wrote the article replied in due course. He'd assumed that only Englishmen read *The London Times*, and said he was highly gratified that a compatriot who lived so far away in India was reading his newspaper. He went on to say that he himself had seen the passage somewhere, and it had made such an impression on him that he had decided to insert it in the *Times*, but that he had no idea whatsoever about *Stars of the Desert* or who wrote it. However, he did suggest that I visit a certain library in London when I was next in England where I might be able to get the information I was seeking.

King Edward VII had views similar to those expressed in *Stars of the Desert*. He was a man far ahead of his time, and a man of liberal views. On his first visit to India in 1875, at the age of thirty four, the heir apparent to the British throne was quick to notice the condescending manner generally assumed by British subjects in India towards Indians. "Just because a man has a black face and a different religion than our own, there is no reason why he should be treated as a brute," the Prince wrote to the Foreign Secretary, less than three weeks after he arrived in Bombay. He was especially displeased by the way the British used the word 'nigger' when referring to Indians. For a Royal on an official visit, it was quite amazing that he was so perceptive.

The British in India, except perhaps the missionaries, did not mix with the Indians. They kept largely to themselves. They had their own Clubs, and had no social intercourse with the Indians. I would suppose that it was this segregation that helped them rule with an air of superiority. British children growing up in India were most likely to develop prejudiced views too, seeing the way their parents behaved towards the subject peoples. Children by nature are, otherwise, 'colour blind'.

That parents had a lot to do with how children reacted to others was brought home to me when I spent a weekend with Col and Mrs Williams in their home in England on my first visit to that country in 1957. They had two children, Janie and Richard. Janie was five or six years old, and Richard a year or so younger. I don't think either of them had seen a coloured man before, living as they did in England.

Janie took to me instantly. She had just started riding lessons, and was eager to show me how she jumped on and got off the pony. The arm of a sofa served as a pony for the demonstration.

I had to go with her wherever she went, and she always led me by the hand saying, "Come, my little man." A couple of times, I took both the children out for walks, and they loved it. When the time came for me to leave, Janie said to her mother, "Mummy, why can't Mr Davidar stay with us always?" Mrs Williams was most tactful. She replied, "I wish he could, darling, but Mr Davidar has work to do and he must go back." Janie was satisfied.

Fifteen years later, I went to England on business. I spent a night with the Williams' again. The children had left home, and Janie was living in London. After a Board meeting that I attended, Col Williams took me home in his car and told me on the way that Janie had been informed that I was visiting them, and that if she wanted to see me again she would have to come over for the night. We got to their house in Sussex late in the afternoon.

I was standing outside after tea when I saw a young girl come through the gate and walk towards the house which was some distance away. She was petite, and as she came closer, I could see that she was also pretty. It was Janie. She was very pleased to see me. It was summer, and there was still some daylight left. Janie said to me, "The last time you were here, you took me for walks. But this time, I am going to drive you around the countryside." And, she did. She chatted away throughout the drive, as though we had not lost contact in the intervening years.

Janie had wonderful parents. Janie wrote to me twenty years after my last visit to give the sad news that her mother had died that year, ten years after Col Williams had passed on. "It is so long (ago) since I saw you, but I remember it like yesterday," her letter began. She went on to give me all the family news. Janie had two daughters, and one of them was a rider like her mother. That year, she had had a "very successful pony year" as Janie called it, and had won some of the major prizes that were on offer in England. The other daughter was an accomplished international mountaineer, and was due in Nepal the following summer.

I joined my Company six years after the country became independent, and was their only Indian Executive. One didn't have to be brilliant to sense that the Indian subordinates, at practically all levels, felt that an Indian was not in the same class as a European. Others connected with the Company also behaved in a similar fashion. I worked on Woodlands division after I had been with the Company for three years. A merchant from Salem who supplied the Company coarse blankets or *cumblies* for the workers leased a godown on the division. I rode past the merchant's warehouse on the motorcycle track which passed in front of it at least twice a day, to and from my bungalow. I also knew the merchant's partner who lived in a portion of the building that housed the store.

Salem is especially noted for its quality mangoes. One day during the mango season, Madden spotted me in the field and stopped for a chat. He asked whether or not I had received my basket of mangoes. I didn't know what he was referring to, and replied in the negative. He just said, "Oh," and left soon afterwards. The next day, I received a copy of the letter that Madden had written to the *cumbly* merchant. In the letter, Madden brought to the notice of the merchant that he had failed to send a basket of mangoes to Mr Davidar, and ordered him to do so forthwith. My basket of mangoes arrived at my doorstep a few days later. I learnt subsequently that the merchant supplied the European Executives in the Company with the choicest Salem mangoes regularly every year. Madden was very fair that way. When he interviewed me for an Assistant Superintendent's job, he told me that while there would be a difference in my pay and that of a European Assistant's, the treatment would be the same. And, Madden kept his word.

Full fifteen years after Independence, some Indians found it difficult to accept that a European could work under an Indian.

As the junior Superintendent in the Company, I once had to act for the Superintendent of Kuduakarnam Estate when he went to England on furlough. Chris Nicholl was the Assistant there.

One afternoon, Chris came to see me about something in the estate office. As we sat chatting, a travelling salesman appeared. He had come from Tamil Nadu where Prohibition was in force. Within a short while, it became all too clear that he had not stinted on his liquid refreshment at lunch. The man had come to sell lubricant for the machines in the factory, which was called *Non-Creep*. Chris asked him why it was called *Non-Creep*. The man replied, "Because it doesn't creep, ha, ha, ha."

He later went next door to Ladrum Estate, where Horrocks was the Superintendent. He informed Horrocks that he had been to Kuduakarnam, and had met the Superintendent there, a tall Englishman. He'd added that an Indian was also in the room, sitting at the big table, directly under the portrait of Churchill, while the Superintendent sat at a side table. Horrocks corrected him instantly. He told the salesman, "The Superintendent on Kuduakarnam is an Indian."

After India became independent, the camaraderie that has developed between the Europeans in India, barring perhaps a few diehards from the days of the Raj, and the Indians is astonishing. The new generation of Indians do not have the kind of complex that my generation laboured under. I think of our children in particular, who were on friendly terms with the children of Chris and Lorraine Nicholl, for instance. And that friendship still continues. Again, parents are mainly responsible for their children's attitude.

In my childhood days in Trichinopoly, I didn't know of any Indian who went abroad. Many Indians travel abroad today, and a good number of Indians live and work in the West. Indians are no longer judged by the tint of their skin but by the quality of their thoughts, so rightly counselled in *Stars of the Desert*. And, Indians can think.

Epilogue

I was fortunate to have been exposed to *The Rubaiyat* of Omar Khayyam, the Persian poet, when I was at university. Some friends could recite the beautiful quatrains backwards. The verse so charmed me that I memorized many of the stanzas myself. One of them read, in part:

The Worldly Hope men set their hearts upon,

Turns Ashes – or it prospers.

I was lucky to have been able to follow the two careers that appealed to me. They prospered for a while, and although they did not turn to ashes, I cannot say with a clear conscience that I was deliriously happy in either of them much of the time. I do not know if many men are happy in the careers that they chose to follow, but I believe as Thoreau observed such a long time ago, that most men do lead lives of quiet desperation in whatever profession they find themselves.

There were periods of bliss in both my jobs. I would be dishonest if I didn't say that my years in planting helped me to acquire the property in The Nilgiris in which I now live in reasonable comfort, despite the odd setback which everybody must experience in life, in some form or the other. I made many friends in both professions, and some of the best friends I have today were tea planters in Kerala, though many of them are now settled in England.

While researching material for my book, one of the first things I did was to look for other titles that might have been written by working planters like myself. My search was largely futile, but I did come across a book called *Assam Planter* (now long out of print) by AR Ramsden, a planter in Assam.

Ramsden was born in Assam. Curiously, there are parallels in our two careers. Ramsden had fought in the First World War, and had resigned his commission in 1922, with the 'uncontrollable desire' to remain in the open air, and go shooting somewhere with a rifle and a dog, both of which he achieved in full measure. Having spent the latter half of his military service in the Indian Army, he spoke Hindustani fluently.

After leaving the Army, Ramsden tried his hand at farming in England for a while, then decided to get into tea planting in Assam. His entry into planting was smoother than mine. The job was his for the asking. Ramsden became a planter in one of the tea plantations on whose Board his father served as a Director.

Ramsden pursued shikar with vigour as he wished to do, but his planting career came to a premature end when he came down with blackwater fever, a severe form of malaria, and had to be repatriated Home. Ramsden was fortunate to have been in planting when it was, more or less, still in the pioneering stages. He kept all kinds of pets including leopard cats, which he swears were untameable and savage. Am I glad that the female leopard cat that I encountered in the company of her two little kittens, at very close range in her own territory, did not mess me up.

Some time after our friends the Lovatts retired and settled in England, Heather wrote to my wife and said that they chose to withdraw more and more from social interactions even prior to leaving India. We did exactly the same. We had other interests like gardening which made life in Peermade tolerable while it lasted. In 1625, Francis Bacon observed, "God Almighty first planted a garden; and, indeed, it is the purest of human pleasures." With a few notable exceptions, the wives of the Indian planters were generally not keen gardeners. There was this senior Indian planter who was engaged by TTE. He and his wife had made their round of visits after arriving in the district, and eventually, came to see us. The man's wife remarked, "All the English ladies we met asked about my garden. Why should I worry when there is a *mali* to look after it?" Indeed.

Heather went on to foretell that when we had our own house and garden "in Coonoor perhaps?" – How did she know we'd come to live in The Nilgiris? – we'd be very happy, where we could live a private life and meet people on our own terms. How very right she was.

When I retired Madden wrote to me. He said, "There's plenty to do in retirement." There certainly is. You are working for yourself, and you get a lot of satisfaction when you see something you have toiled for bear fruit. I am now into my thirtieth year of retirement, and I have been busy much of the time. When King Edward VIII was the Prince of Wales, he went to inaugurate a public project one day, to fulfil a Royal obligation. As he got out of the royal limousine, he overheard a bystander, a man, remark sarcastically, "Idle rich." The Prince stopped in his tracks, turned to the man and said, "Rich maybe, but not so idle." That's me, I've never been idle. There has always been something to do, some problem to sort out.

Both TTE and my Company, SITE, were two of the earliest Companies to set up business in the district, in 1897. Exactly eighty years later, in 1977, I handed over charge of my Company to the newly-appointed Managing Agents. When I left, the Company was at the peak of prosperity, the tea in good heart as even the No.1 of the Managing Agents admitted to me. The Company's coffers overflowed.

It was a good time to go.

∽

Appendix
(A Brief History of Tea)

Several delightful legends surround the origin of tea as a beverage.

The oldest known story dates back to 2737 BC. Even in those distant days, the Chinese Emperor Shen Nung (or Chen Nung) believed in the highest standards of hygiene, and always boiled his water before drinking it. One evening of that year, when touring his kingdom, the Emperor's servants were boiling water while he was resting at camp. Some leaves from the twigs that the servants were using for the fire drifted up and fell into the water. The Emperor became intrigued by the aroma that emanated from the water that was boiling. He drank it out of curiosity, and found it was flavoursome and refreshing that he said at the time that it gave one vigour of body, contentment of mind and determination of purpose. He declared the drink as T'e (pronounced tay), a divine healer. He was later to extol the virtues of tea in most enthusiastic terms. In brief, this is what he said: "Tea is better than wine for it leadeth not to intoxication, neither does it cause a man to say foolish things and repent thereof in his sober moments. It is better than water for it does not carry disease; neither does it act like poison as water does when it contains foul and rotten matter."

Japanese folklore attributes the discovery of tea to an Indian Buddhist monk, Daruma or Bodhidharma, the founder of Zen Buddhism (which was introduced to Japan from China in the twelfth century). Daruma went to China from India to preach the message of Lord Buddha. While meditating near Nanking he fell asleep, though he had vowed he would stay awake for nine years until he finished his prayers. He was so disgusted with himself that he tore off his eyelids and threw them away. Where the eyelids fell, a strange evergreen plant came up. Daruma plucked the leaves, boiled them in water and when he drank the brew, he found it could banish sleep. Thus was tea as a drink born.

Another legend, not so gruesome, has it that the monk Daruma had vowed that he would meditate for seven years without sleeping, but after five years he began to feel drowsy. To keep himself awake, he stretched out his hand, plucked a few leaves from a nearby bush and chewed on them. He immediately felt so refreshed, that he was able to complete the remaining two years of his meditation without any difficulty. The leaves came from a tea bush.

I know from personal experience that drinking tea banishes sleep. When I was in college in Madras, we were given a month's study leave before our final university examinations. In order to stay awake and study during much of the night, most of us who lived in the college hostel were supplied tea at regular intervals in our rooms by the Mess servants. God knows I needed to be more awake than most.

❖❖❖

The Chinese were the earliest drinkers of the beverage. It is believed that tea originated in China in the fourth century AD. As early as the eighth century (780 AD), the Chinese scholar, Lu Yu, was asked by Chinese tea merchants to write a book about tea to boost their sales. Lu Yu's book was called the *Ch'a Ching* (in three volumes) which may be roughly translated as *The Tea Book*. The book covered all aspects of tea from its growing to its making and drinking. According to Lu Yu, drinking tea was very popular during the flamboyant T'ang dynasty (620 – 907 AD). Several benefits were attributed to drinking tea. Among them, tea was believed to have a cooling effect, and one was advised to drink only tea four or five times a day when feeling hot, thirsty, depressed or suffering from headache, eye-ache, fatigue of the four limbs and pains in the joints. Generally, boiled water was meant to quench thirst, wine to drown sorrow and tea to avoid drowsiness.

China remained the only producer and consumer of tea for centuries. The Dutch East India Company was the first major importer of tea into Europe from China around 1606. People began to drink tea in Amsterdam, London and Paris, but it remained an expensive luxury. Only Europe's high society could afford it. From the year 1669, the British East India Company (which was formed in 1600 and went on to become the most powerful trading Company in the world) started importing tea into England. However, the first public sale of tea took place in London much earlier, in 1657, in a coffee house owned by Thomas Garraway who advertised twenty four maladies that the consumption of tea could be expected to cure. According to him, there was hardly any organ in the human body that did not benefit from the ingestion of tea. I do not know when advertising as a business came into existence, but Garraway instinctively knew what advertising was all about. Its reminds one of the little schoolboy who wrote on the blackboard, "Johnny is a passionate little devil." The teacher, a lady, was not amused, and asked Johnny to stay back when the class gave over as she wanted to speak to him. It took a long time for Johnny to emerge from behind the closed doors. His classmates, who had been anxiously waiting outside, crowded around him and wanted to know what had happened. Johnny said simply, "I am not saying anything except that it sure pays to advertise."

Thomas Lipton, a grocer from Glasgow, whose name will forever be associated with tea knew the value of advertising and used it to maximum effect to become an extremely wealthy man. He was courted by the elite of the time (who normally shunned the trading community), and even counted King Edward VII as one of his friends. Lipton who was knighted by Queen Victoria, became the owner of four tea estates in

Ceylon, quite serendipitously, at just the right time, and he made several millions.

Following the public sale of tea by Garraway, it appealed to everyone. The British Government promptly slapped a punitive tax on it in 1660. As a result, the consumption of tea continued to be restricted to the wealthy, and beer remained the popular drink of choice in England for quite a while longer. Queen Elizabeth I was known to drink as much as a gallon of beer at breakfast. Again, as a direct corollary of the heavy tax imposed on the import of tea into England, the populace devised ways and means to avoid paying it. Smuggling became widespread, and traders in London encouraged the practice. In order to compete with the contraband stuff, a large cut in the tax became inevitable. This came about with the promulgation of the Commutation Act by Parliament in 1784. Too late, perhaps.

Interestingly, English immigrants to America took the tea-drinking habit with them. Tea was originally introduced into America by the Dutch in the seventeenth century, and much like in Europe, initially only the upper-class families in Philadelphia and Boston could afford to drink it because of its prohibitive cost. When England slapped on a heavy tea tax, passed by Parliament and called the Tea Act, it was resented by the New England colonists, and there were strident calls for the boycott of the beverage. On 16 December 1773, patriotic Americans from the Saint Andrews Masonic Lodge in Boston, calling themselves 'Sons of Liberty' dressed up as Mohawk Indians to avoid detection, boarded three East India Company ships anchored at Boston harbour (*The Beaver, The Eleanor* and *The Dartmouth*), and threw three hundred and forty chests of tea into the harbour. This incident came to be popularly known as the Boston Tea Party. Not unnaturally, this defiant act attracted British reprisals and resulted in the Battle of Bunker Hill, which eventually led to the Declaration of Independence in 1776. Tea had started the revolution, but lost the war because the Americans turned to drinking coffee.

China continued to be the only producer of tea, and started placing low-quality tea on the market, to partly meet the ever-rising demand in Europe, and particularly in Britain. To add to the woes of the British, China insisted on payment for its tea in hard cash, in silver.

In order to pay for its tea, Britain first exported cotton from Bengal in India to China. But China soon started manufacturing its own cotton which was better in quality and cheaper than the imported Indian cotton. Therefore, a new strategy had to be devised.

In 1758, Parliament gave the East India Company the monopoly to produce opium in India, and the cultivation of opium by private enterprise was totally forbidden. While import of opium into China was banned, the Portuguese traded illegally in the substance as it was a lucrative business. The British wrested the opium trade from them in 1773, and started exporting large quantities of the banned substance into China. By the 1830s, opium was being pumped into China in an unstoppable flood. When all efforts by the Chinese authorities to curb the menace failed, they burnt a whole year's supply of opium in a huge bonfire, and took drastic action against the British and the Chinese who were involved in the trade. By an edict of the Emperor, Canton, the only port that was open for trading, was closed. Britain was incensed and the first Opium War of 1839 – 1842 was declared. The superior British Navy pounded the Chinese fortifications, and subdued them into submission. The Chinese Government was forced to make humiliating concessions to Britain. Several ports, including Canton, were reopened for trading in opium once again. Until then, Canton was the only port where tea was brought in chests from distant regions in the north, but no European was allowed to enter the city itself. However, subduing China was not going to make for a permanent solution to the problem, and the British realized that they had to start a tea industry of their own. The only impediment was that hardly anything was known about how to grow and manufacture tea. The Chinese kept it a closely-guarded secret, and any one divulging it to outsiders faced extreme punishment, even death.

As early as 1778, Sir Joseph Banks, the eminent botanist of the time, and Director of Kew Gardens in London, had advised the East India Company that the Indian climate between certain parallels of latitude (between twenty six and thirty), was most suitable for the cultivation of tea. The East India Company which had the monopoly of the tea trade from 1669 was not seriously interested in taking his advice as their tea business with China continued to flourish. In 1833, however, the East India Company lost its monopoly in the tea trade by an act of Parliament, which made it imperative that alternatives for sourcing the commodity be found. Sir William Bentinck, the then Governor-General in India, set up the Tea Committee in 1834 to gather information on tea cultivation in the country. The Bruce brothers came on the scene at about this time, and the tea industry in India was born.

∿

Acknowledgements

A part from George and Usha Joseph, I am most grateful to my children, David and Ruth, without whose constant encouragement, help and support, this book would not have seen the light of day. When the job was finally done, my son did a magnificent job of editing, and my daughter willingly undertook the onerous task of dealing with the publication of the book.

George and Usha told me that a computer would be a great help in the work that I was to embark upon. I bought one not knowing that it would need skill to operate. The family pitched in to help. With great patience David and Ruth and their respective spouses, Rachna Singh and Rajendra Swamy, helped me learn how to use it when I started writing. To all four of them, my grateful thanks. Pinki Virani was one of the many who saw me through the difficult time after my wife's death, for which I am deeply indebted to her. Knowing my love for the English language, she kept me in good humour by sending me quirky new ways of expression like the saying from the International English Language Testing System (IELTS), 'It is fruitless to attempt to indoctrinate a superannuated canine with innovative manoeuvres', which simply means in the English we know 'You cannot teach an old dog new tricks'. It was not too easy but I learnt a few tricks, enough to cope.

To my friends in The United Planters' Association of Southern India (UPASI) in Coonoor, The Nilgiris, I cannot be too grateful. Ullas Menon, the Secretary General, could not do enough to be of assistance. Dr B Radhakrishnan of the Scientific Department found just the maps I needed for this book, and they adorn the inside of the front and back covers. Besides, Dr Radhakrishnan provided other information on tea that I wanted, while JB Hudson, his predecessor in office, got me going with this project. Anasuya Murthy, the librarian, cheerfully helped me in my search for the required material, and J Durairaj graciously supplied the cover photograph.

When my very old friend EK Joseph was the President of UPASI (2000 – 2001), I told him that I was thinking of writing a book about my life in tea. He generously asked Ullas Menon to help me. You couldn't ask for a better friend.

Two other former colleagues, Ravi Mathews and DP Joshua, were always willing to supply information about my old Company whenever I asked for it. To them, I say a very big 'Thank You'.

To Yasmin Kothavala who told me about the Gujarati saying that appears in this book and explained its meaning, and to Sunita Shastry who identified the author (Victor Hugo) of the quotation reproduced in the Epigraph, I offer my sincere gratitude.

I am grateful to my friends in the United Kingdom: Chris Nicholl who was most enthusiastic when he heard of my intended mission, and generously offered to lend me the papers he had from his planting days; Alex York who thought it was a good idea; Victor Whyte who responded promptly to the questions I asked him; and, Eddie Taylor who telephoned me from Scotland to wish me luck.

I owe a debt of gratitude to Srinivas Reddy who not only procured and installed my computer for me, but who was also always willing to come to my aid whenever I sought his assistance in the use of the machine.

Margie Vaz has been asking me for some time to write a book, so I'm sure she will be pleased that I have done so.

The Book of Indian Birds by the renowned ornithologist, Salim Ali, gave me the exact colouring of small minivets, and from *The Book of Indian Animals* by SH Prater, former Curator of the

Bombay Natural History Society, I learnt that the leopard cat is a nocturnal animal.

The photographs that appear in the book have been selected from my private collection.

Finally and importantly, I would like to thank S Muthiah for his helpful editorial suggestions, and my publisher, KS Padmanabhan of EastWest Books (Madras) Private Limited for everything he has done to make the publication of this book possible.

∽

Select Bibliography

Ali, Salim, (1961), *The Book of Indian Birds*, 6th Ed, Bombay Natural History Society, Bombay

Burgess, Anthony, (Ed), (1992), *The Book of Tea*, Flammarion

Goodwin, Jason, (1993), *The Gunpowder Gardens*, Vintage, London

Griffiths, Sir Percival, (1967), *The History of the Indian Tea Industry*, Weidenfeld and Nicholson, London

Lazarus, EC, (Ed), (1881), *The Tea Cyclopedia*, 10, Hare Street, Calcutta

Lovatt, Heather & de Jong, Peter, (1993), *Above the Heron's Pool*, Putney, London

Mcfarlane, Alan & Mcfarlane, Iris, (2003), *Green Gold: The Empire of Tea*, Ebury Press, London

Muthiah, S, (1993), *A Planting Century*, Affiliated East-West Press Pvt Ltd, New Delhi

Prater, SH, (1965), *The Book of Indian Animals*, 2nd Ed, Bombay Natural History Society, Bombay

Ramsden AR, (1945), *Assam Planter*, John Gifford Ltd, London

Scott, JM, (1964), *The Tea Story*, William Heinemann Ltd, London

Speer, SG, (Ed), (1953), *UPASI 1893 – 1953*, The United Planters' Association of Southern India, The Nilgiris

The Central Travancore Planters' Association, *Centenary Souvenir 1874 – 1974*, Kerala

The New Penguin Dictionary of Quotations, (1993), Rvsd Ed, Penguin Books, England

The Planters' Chronicle (Planting Memoirs), Vol. LXXIV, December 1979, No:12